THESE DOGS DON'T HUNT

THE DEMOCRATS' WAR ON GUNS

THESE DOGS DON'T HUNT

THE DEMOCRATS' WAR ON GUNS

ALAN GOTTLIEB
&
DAVE WORKMAN

MERRIL PRESS
BELLEVUE, WASHINGTON

These Dogs Don't Hunt © 2008

Merril Press

All Rights Reserved.

These Dogs Don't Hunt is published by

Merril Press, P.O. Box 1682, Bellevue, WA 98009

www.merrilpress.com

Phone: 425-454-7008

Distributed to the book trade by

Midpoint Trade Books, 27 W. 20th Street, New York, N.Y. 10011

www.midpointtradebooks.com

Phone: 212-727-0190

FIRST EDITION

LIBRARY OF CONGRESS CATALOGING-IN-PUBLICATION DATA

GOTTLIEB, ALAN M.
    THESE DOGS DON'T HUNT : THE DEMOCRATS' WAR ON GUNS / BY ALAN GOTTLIEB AND DAVE
WORKMAN. -- 1ST ED.
        P. CM.
    ISBN 978-0-936783-55-0
    1. GUN CONTROL--UNITED STATES. 2. FIREARMS--LAW AND LEGISLATION-
-UNITED
    STATES. 3. DEMOCRATIC PARTY (U.S.) I. WORKMAN, DAVE. II. TITLE. III.
TITLE:
    THESE DOGS DO NOT HUNT.
    HV7436.G676 2008
    363.330973--DC22

                                    2008023752

PRINTED IN THE UNITED STATES OF AMERICA

'I MIGHT AS WELL INTRODUCE MYSELF...'

She is unabashedly in favor of strict gun control, yet she claims to "support" the Second Amendment right of an American citizen to keep and bear arms. She has, according to Your Guide to Civil Liberties, a 72 percent lifetime rating from the American Civil Liberties Union – an organization that, gun rights activists quickly argue, believes there are only nine amendments in the Bill of Rights – while earning an "F" rating from the National Rifle Association.

She lobbied on behalf of her husband's gun control efforts while serving as First Lady, and she has announced support for such measures as one-gun-a-month and raising the minimum age to legally own a handgun to 21 years. She also believes that all new handgun purchases should be registered.

Critics in the gun rights community are quick to stress that "she never met a piece of gun control legislation she didn't fall in love with." She has supported the ban on semiautomatic sport utility rifles and its unsuccessful renewal, and in June 2000 when she was campaigning for her first term as junior senator from New York, she was quoted by CNN stating, "I stand in support of this common sense legislation to license everyone who wishes to purchase a gun," backing a bill sponsored by perennial anti-gun New York Senator Charles Schumer that would have mandated a state-issued gun license in order to purchase a handgun.

According to a memoir, and several statements on the campaign trail, she once shot a banded duck while on what may have been the only hunting trip she ever took, with a man identified by reporter John Brummett, writing for the Arkansas New Bureau on August 23, 2007, as the late Dr. Frank Kumpuris of Little Rock and his two sons, Drew and Dean. Killing the duck landed her in hot water with her daughter and only child, Chelsea, the report noted, who would not speak to her for days.

Beginning early in 2007, she started running hard to become the first female president of the United States, and some critics suggest that she had been involved in this campaign since long before she left the White House to move to New York, running in 2000 for the Senate seat being vacated at the time by the late Daniel Patrick Moynihan.

Hillary Diane Rodham Clinton is a woman that adoring fans love, and political enemies love to hate, and she epitomizes what may be wrong with far too many Democrat politicians, party leaders, activists and advisors in the United States today: They offer lip service to the Second Amendment, and claim to "support" the individual right of the people to keep and bear arms, but in practice, they have a collective track record on this particular civil right that is abysmal.

Indeed, gun owners in the United States look at Hillary Clinton's history and they see the stereotype of *all* Democrat politicians, a group elected to serve that has presumed instead to reign.

The list is long and includes Clinton's fellow Senators Barack Obama, Dianne Feinstein, Charles Schumer, Barbara Boxer, Patty Murray, Maria Cantwell, Joseph Biden, Frank Lautenberg, Christopher Dodd, Carl Levin, Edward M. Kennedy, Dick Durbin and John Kerry. It would include too many members of the House of Representatives, led by anti-gun House Speaker Nancy Pelosi of California, to list in these pages, plus governors like Jon Corzine of New Jersey, Rod Blagojevich of Illinois and Jim Doyle of Wisconsin. And one cannot forget mayors including Washington, D.C.'s Adrian Fenty, Chicago's Richard Daley, Philadelphia's Michael Nutter, Seattle's Greg Nickels, San Francisco's Gavin Newsom and New Orleans' Ray Nagin.

All have enjoyed popularity among their constituents, and some have achieved adoration on a national scale – Obama, of course, being the text book example of a "rising star" to which far too many in the press have adoringly and unashamedly been clinging throughout much of the 2008 Democratic presidential primary race – but perhaps none of them have held the same kind of aura for as long a period as Hillary Clinton. Depending upon one's perspective, she either proved herself to not be a quitter, and instead a bare knuckles political brawler, or she proved herself to be even more self-absorbed about fulfilling some sort of pre-ordained "destiny" than her husband, and as a result she just won't go away.

Yet one cannot look at her story without looking at the path that the Democratic Party has followed over the past two generations, a party that has walked away from the populism of Harry Truman to embrace the condescending elitism of people like John Edwards.

The other half of what former President Bill Clinton said would be "two for the price of one" when he was running for election in 1992, Hillary Diane Rodham was born in Chicago, Illinois on October 26, 1947 – the 66th anniversary of the famed Gunfight at the OK Corral in Tombstone, Arizona in 1881 – the daughter of Hugh Ellsworth Rodham and Dorothy Emma Howell Rodham, according to an extensive biography on Wikipedia.

Raised in suburban Park Ridge, Illinois, Hillary Rodham enrolled in

Wellesley College in 1965, majoring in political science and during her freshman year, serving as president of the Young Republicans chapter there. She was the first student to speak during commencement exercises at Wellesley in 1969, and indication of where she intended to go, eventually becoming the first female partner at the Rose Law Firm in Little Rock, Arkansas, and the first woman elected to the United States Senate from the state of New York in 2000.

But it was at Wellesley, according to the Wikipedia biography, where Hillary Rodham's politics began taking a turn to the Left. As it did with so many members of her generation, the war in Vietnam affected her ideology, as did the civil rights movement. She quit as Young Republicans president, and reportedly stated that she had "a mind conservative and a heart liberal," according to Carl Bernstein's book *A Woman In Charge*.

She attended and graduated from Yale Law School in 1973 and then became, for a time in 1974, a Congressional legal counsel during the Watergate investigation when she served on the impeachment inquiry staff, according to Wikipedia, "advising the House Committee on the Judiciary" on what would have become the impeachment of Republican President Richard Nixon. This was no small irony, since, as a 13-year-old child in a politically conservative family, her Wikipedia biography notes, she had actually helped uncover vote fraud in Chicago's South Side after the 1960 presidential election; fraud that contributed to the election of John F. Kennedy over Nixon to the White House. A few years later, still as a teenager, she would volunteer in the 1964 presidential campaign of Arizona Senator Barry Goldwater. She was at one time also president of a fan club for teen heartthrob Fabian, according to Fox News.

Coincidentally, the Senate Watergate Committee's chief minority counsel was attorney Fred Dalton Thompson, who would later become a character actor and United States Senator from Tennessee before stepping down in 2002. Thompson would later run for president of the United States as a Republican at the same time Hillary Rodham Clinton was running as a Democrat, though Thompson stepped out of the race in January 2008 after weak showings in early primary elections and caucuses.

It was in 1969, according to her official White House biography as First Lady, that she met Bill Clinton at Yale. By his version, the biography states, the two met in the library and she had noticed him staring at her. Clinton's recollection of the meeting was that she walked up to him and said, "If you're going to keep staring at me, I might as well introduce myself."

Partners in Politics, Partners in Life

After that meeting, according to the White House biography, Hillary Rodham and William Jefferson Clinton "were soon inseparable – partners in moot court, political campaigns, and matters of the heart."

And even though, years later after making a somewhat condescending remark about country singer Tammy Wynette and her song "Stand By Your Man," and cookie baking – for which she later apologized – Hillary Rodham Clinton has indeed stood by her man through some remarkably sordid events, the so-called "Bimbo eruptions" involving various women that culminated with the Monica Lewinsky affair and his impeachment by the U.S. House of Representatives for lying under oath, though the Senate failed to convict.

Some might argue that Hillary stood by Bill – her leaving the White House to run for Senate in New York and establish residency in that state while he remained in the White House finishing out his term might have been the closest thing to a legal separation – as much out of political savvy as love. She knew even then that she would run for president, and she also knew that, despite his character flaws, Bill Clinton is a campaigner's dream for his ability to please a crowd and raise campaign funds.

And it might be for Bill Clinton a kind of penance for his philandering that caused his wife and the mother of his only child such high profile national and international embarrassment. In Arkansas, where Clinton grew up and got his political start, it would not be unheard of for other couples with that kind of history to end their marriage with a "12-gauge divorce."

But Hillary Rodham Clinton hadn't come this far just to throw it all away by wasting good buckshot on a no-good hubby. Her ascent to prominence had been years in the making.

According to Hillary's Wikipedia biography, she and Bill started dating in the spring of 1971 and that summer she went to California to intern for the law firm of Treuhaft, Walker and Burnstein on child custody cases. Treuhaft had been a communist in the 1950s and the law firm was known for its support of radical causes, civil rights and some constitutional issues. This may have been a turning point for Hillary, because the following year, in 1972, she accompanied Bill to Texas where they campaigned for George McGovern, the Democratic presidential nominee whose crushing defeat by Richard Nixon did not deter either from politics.

She earned a Juris Doctor degree from Yale in 1973, Wikipedia notes, and turned down Bill Clinton's first proposal of marriage, instead starting a year of post-graduate study on children at the Yale Child Study Center. She served as an attorney with the anti-gun rights Children's Defense Fund in Cambridge, Massachusetts and authored a paper titled *Children Under the Law* that was published in the *Harvard Educational Review*.

Her attention and interest in children's issues might have been at the root of a strategy born years later in the gun control movement to sell any and every restrictive gun control proposal as being "for the children."

Only months later, she was working on the Nixon /Watergate scandal, culminating in Nixon's historic resignation in 1974.

And according to the Wikipedia biography, it was at that time that a Democrat political consultant named Betsey Wright saw in Rodham the makings of a future senator or even president. Wright would later become chief of staff for Bill Clinton when he served as governor of Arkansas, and deputy chair of the 1992 Clinton/Gore campaign.

Hillary Rodham passed the bar exam in Arkansas but failed on her first try to pass the bar exam for the District of Columbia, and that apparently contributed to her decision to head for Arkansas in August 1974 where Bill Clinton was teaching law at the University of Arkansas, Fayetteville School of Law and running for the U.S. House of Representatives, a race he lost.

Moving to Arkansas must have been something of a culture shock for the Illinois-raised, Yale-educated Hillary Rodham. In case Bill had forgotten to mention it, Arkansas is gun country, and while the state has its share of culture, it also has its share of conservative firearms owners who would no sooner shake hands with a anti-gun rights Yale graduate than they would a rattlesnake.

Drive in any direction from Little Rock, and you are in real estate far more comfortable with the NRA than with the NOW. Many Arkansans would later quietly admit, in the 1990s after Bill Clinton was elected president that they voted for him in 1992 just to get him out of the statehouse.

In the summer of 1975, Bill and Hillary bought a house in Fayetteville and they were married in the living room of that house in a Methodist ceremony on October 11. She reportedly kept her maiden name to keep their professional lives separate.

Bill Clinton's march up the political ladder started in November 1976 when he was elected attorney general of Arkansas. The Clintons moved from Fayetteville to Little Rock, where Hillary joined the Rose Law Firm, where she worked *pro bono* in child advocacy cases, and also worked on intellectual property and patent infringement law, her biography notes. She also co-founded the Arkansas Advocates for Children and Families, further reinforcing her image and reputation as a child advocate.

While Bill was running for attorney general, Hillary had worked for anti-gun rights Gov. Jimmy Carter in his bid to become president, as a campaign coordinator in Indiana. Carter subsequently named her to the Legal Services Corporation board of directors in 1977, where she served until 1981.

Ups and Downs

In 1978, Bill Clinton decided to climb up the political ladder another rung, and he successfully ran for his first term as Arkansas governor with Hillary at his side. That term ended in 1981 in defeat, but true to his later image as "the comeback kid," Clinton ran again in 1982 and won, this time staying in office until 1992 when he made his bid for the White House.

It was during her first stint as First Lady of Arkansas that Hillary Rodham Clinton gave birth to the couple's only child, Chelsea, on February 27, 1980. This child would never know her parents outside of a political environment.

During her time as First Lady in Arkansas, Hillary was a full partner at the Rose Law Firm, and she also served as chair of the Rural Health Advisory Committee during Bill's first term. While she made what would later become a very controversial investment in cattle futures, turning a $1,000 contract purchase into a $100,000 profit after ten months, the Clintons lost money in a real estate venture called the Whitewater Development Corporation.

In 1983, Hillary Clinton was named Arkansas Woman of the Year, and in 1984, she was named Arkansas Mother of the Year. There would be more honors. She chaired the Commission on Women for the American Bar Association from 1987 to 1991, and in 1988 and again in 1991, she was identified as being among the 100 most influential attorneys in the country by the National Law Journal.

She also served on several boards, and once even considered a run for Arkansas governor when it appeared Bill was preparing to step down, but ultimately he did run for a final term, apparently after private polling on Hillary's popularity was discouraging.

But then came 1992 and Bill Clinton's run for the White House brought Hillary into the national spotlight as perhaps no other bride of a candidate had ever been. The press seemed to adore Bill Clinton, and they made lots more hay with maverick independent Ross Perot (and his running mate, James Stockdale), who was in the race, then out of it, and then back in again, garnering more than 19 million votes (no electoral college votes) and many believe he drained the majority of those votes away from the Republican ticket, thus handing Clinton the election, though it was no landslide.

The Clinton/Gore ticket pulled 44.9 million votes for 43 percent of the total vote and 370 electoral votes, while the incumbent ticket of Bush and Vice President Dan Quayle garnered 39.1 million votes for 37.4 percent of the total ballots cast.

It was enough to send the Clintons to Washington, D.C. and if anyone had previously wondered where Hillary Rodham Clinton stood on the issues, the curiosity vanished very soon. Hillary, according to her own memoir, Living History, became the first First Lady to have an office in the White House's West Wing, breaking a tradition that had previous First Ladies' offices in the East Wing, perhaps the first real signal about her expectations – some would call it lust – for power and authority. It was just one aspect of the perception, and perhaps the reality, that Hillary and Bill Clinton were, in many ways, co-presidents.

Conservative commentators maintain that she pressured Bill to name women to at least half of his cabinet positions, resulting in the appointment of anti-gun rights Janet Reno as attorney general and Madeleine Albright as Secretary of State. Critics of the Clinton presidency have contended that neither was qualified, and Reno's botched handling of the Branch Davidian siege at Waco that resulted in the fiery deaths of dozens of people when the Mt. Carmel compound burned to the ground seemed to affirm their criticisms.

Late in Bill Clinton's presidency, when Reno ordered federal officers to seize young Cuban immigrant Elian Gonzales and turn him over to his father for a flight back to the Communist island, the public was outraged.

Someone said that the Clinton presidency could be framed between two bookend photographs, the image of a burning Mt. Carmel at one end, and the image of a federal agent grabbing the Gonzales child at gunpoint from the arms of the terrified fisherman who had originally rescued him.

In between, Bill Clinton would become known as the man who pushed through the Brady Law – sections of which were later found to be unconstitutional by the Supreme Court – and the following year, the so-called "assault weapons ban" that didn't really ban anything but simply prevented the manufacture and importation of specific firearms and full-capacity magazines over a ten-year period.

It was Bill who pushed those laws and signed them, but in the background, Hillary emerged as a staunch supporter of these gun laws and other anti-gun proposals.

It was Clinton's support for those laws, pressuring a Democrat-controlled Congress, that led to the disastrous 1994 mid-term elections when more than 50 members of Congress who had voted for both measures were thrown out of office, replaced by Republicans who had run and gotten support from the firearms community on the presumption that there would be no more gun control legislation. For the rest of Bill Clinton's administration, and well into the subsequent administration of George W. Bush, Republicans controlled both houses of Congress, but failed to deliver on any promises, real or imagined that certain gun laws would be repealed. The Republican majority, and gun shy Democrats, allowed the ban on semi-autos to expire, but that's not the same thing as actually repealing a repugnant federal statute.

'I support the Second Amendment...'

Long before she "officially" began running for president, even before she "officially" began running for Moynihan's soon-to-be-vacated New York senate seat, Hillary Diane Rodham Clinton began emerging as an outspoken supporter of gun control laws, following a pattern that has become well established among Democrats on the Far Left.

More recently, since being elected to the Senate, she voted against legislation to prevent the kind of outrageous gun confiscations that were undertaken by police in New Orleans in 2005 following Hurricane Katrina; an unusual position for an attorney concerned about civil rights because these gun seizures were conducted without legal authority, without warrants and without due process.

It was that program of confiscation which brought the Second Amendment Foundation and the National Rifle Association together as partners in a landmark federal lawsuit that resulted in a ruling that the seizures were illegal and unconstitutional. One would think an attorney the caliber of Hillary Rodham Clinton would have taken notice of the precedent and cast her Senate vote accordingly, but it appears that in her world view, one of America's most fundamental individual civil rights is expendable in the quest for political correctness.

Hillary apparently doesn't *hate* firearms. She shot a gun as a child on a trip with her family to their summer vacation cabin on Lake Winola in Pennsylvania, about 20 miles northwest from Scranton, according to a story that appeared in the Allentown *Morning Call* that appeared in early September 2007. And then there was that duck hunt with Dr. Kumpuris mentioned earlier in this chapter.

But her experience with firearms may be similar to that of other politicians who believe in gun control: "I can handle a firearm safely and responsibly, but everyone else is suspect and needs to be screened."

This attitude was perhaps best described by NRA Executive Vice President Wayne LaPierre in an essay that appeared in the February 2008 issue of the NRA magazine *America's First Freedom*. He called it "Hillary's wink-and-nod lip service to the Second Amendment."

When Hillary was interviewed by the *Des Moines Register* in October 2007 while campaigning early for the upcoming Iowa Caucus, she insisted that she does "support" the Second Amendment…"But I also believe in smart laws that keep guns out of the hands of criminals and terrorists."

It was not unlike other pronouncements, made by Clinton while she was still First Lady. Her anti-gun philosophy emerged forcefully following the Columbine High School massacre in spring of 1999 in Littleton, Colorado.

During a June 4 appearance on ABC's Good Morning America, according to the website GoVote.com, she offered this advice: "If you own a gun… make sure it's locked up and stored without the ammunition. In fact, make it stored where the ammunition is stored separately. We've made some progress in the last several years with the Brady Bill and some of the bans on assault weapons, but we have a lot of work to do."

On July 5, Hillary told the National Education Association in Orlando, Florida that "We have to do everything possible to keep guns out of the hands of children, and we need to stand firm on behalf of the sensible gun control legislation that passed the Senate and then was watered down in the House.

"It does not make sense for us at this point in our history," she said, "to turn our backs on the reality that there are too many guns and too many children have access to those guns-and we have to act to prevent that."

Ten days later, speaking at a forum at the South Side Middle School in New York's Nassau County, she again spoke in support of tougher gun control measures.

"We will not make progress on a sensible gun control agenda unless the entire American public gets behind it," she reportedly stated. "It is really important for each of you [children] to make sure you stay away from guns. If you have guns in your home, tell your parents to keep them away from you and your friends and your little brothers and sisters."

This was not the first time Hillary or other gun control proponents have made gun control a child safety issue, but she began stressing the theme after Columbine.

And in a July 31, 1999 press release, she remarked, "I hope we will come together as a nation and do whatever it takes to keep guns away from people who have no business with them."

But as with other gun control proponents, determining who these people "who have no business with" firearms is usually an all-encompassing process, in which all citizens must go through background checks and waiting periods, even if they sell or give a firearm to a family member or personal friend, perhaps face licensing and registration requirements, and other restrictions.

Somewhere in this process – NRA's LaPierre points an accusing finger at political operatives Jonathan Cowan and Jim Kessler for being the strategists – Hillary became a leader in the effort to change the rhetoric of the gun ban extremist movement. Instead of talking about *gun control,* she and others shifted the dialogue to *gun safety.* After all, who would not support a firearm safety campaign?

Every new gun control proposal became "sensible gun safety legislation." Irrational gun control objectives, such as "gun free zones" became "common-sense gun safety" measures. It was a savvy, calculated exercise in political semantics that initially paid off by convincing a great many Americans that the gun control movement was primarily concerned with safety, not confiscatory regulation.

The creation in late 2001-early 2002 of a front organization called Americans for Gun Safety (AGS), an outfit that was financed by billionaire gun hater Andrew McKelvey, has given Hillary Clinton and others like her plenty of cover to pander gun safety in the form of increasingly restrictive and intrusive gun control legislation. AGS was headed up by Cowan, a former assistant to anti-gunner Andrew Cuomo, when he served as HUD Secretary under Bill Clinton; Kessler, who had worked for anti-gun Sen. Schumer, and Matt Bennett, a Clinton White House aide. At the time of this writing, Cuomo

13

was attorney general for the State of New York.

When it became obvious that AGS really was nothing but a thinly-disguised gun control organization, and the AGS Foundation likewise more interested in controlling and even banning guns than it is in gun safety, a transformation occurred with the result being that AGS and its Foundation became a new front group called Third Way, under control of the same three men. Cowan is now Third Way's president, Bennett is vice president for public affairs and Kessler is vice president for policy.

As self-proclaimed "progressives," these gun control extremists have promoted and supported every form of radical gun control on the map, and LaPierre predicted in his magazine article that if Hillary Rodham Clinton were to ascend to the presidency, all three of these men, and perhaps even Cuomo, would once again be right back in the White House helping to determine the second Clinton Administration's gun control policy, and it would not be friendly to the nation's 80 million gun owners.

Many observers noted during the back-and-forth horse race to the 2008 Democratic nomination that even if Hillary were not to gain the nomination and become the first female president of the United States – a "coronation" that critics believe she anticipated since well before her election to the U.S. Senate in November 2000 and her subsequent departure as First Lady in January 2001 – she would remain in the Senate, where she is seen as one of the leading enemies of gun rights.

It was not outside the realm of plausibility that a defeat in the campaign for the Democratic nomination would leave Hillary blaming, at least in part, gun owners who – despite support from Democrat gun owners in places like Ohio and Pennsylvania – have long considered her the enemy.

One need only recall what the anti-gun New York Times said of then-First Lady Hillary Rodham Clinton in an April 8, 1999 piece: "Mrs. Clinton, who is considering running for Senate from New York, where gun control is popular, has also been more forceful than the president in directly taking on the powerful gun lobby."

There is no doubt in the minds of gun rights activists that, despite her numerous presidential campaign remarks to the contrary, she has been salivating for a re-match.

Two

WE ARE THE PARTY OF GUN CONTROL

Every iceberg has its proverbial tip, and both Hillary Diane Rodham Clinton and Barack Hussein Obama certainly qualify as the most visible twin peak of a deep, and Titanic-ally dangerous political iceberg that is the Democratic Party when it comes to gun control.

Yes, the entire country has heard Democrats from one coast to the other insisting that they support gun rights, that they are gun owners and are not out to grab anyone's guns. Democrats who are truly and vehemently opposed to the notion of an individual right to own a gun have learned to keep silent unless they are in politically safe districts, so over time, their constituents tend to forget or simply overlook their records on the gun rights issue. However, when one considers the consistent attitude of condescension that leading Democrats have repeatedly displayed toward rural Americans, particularly those with firearms and who share other conservative values, there can be no plausible deniability that Democrats leading the party dislike firearms.

It is amply proven in their voting records. Thanks to a marvelous website OnTheIssues.org, anybody with a home computer and access to the Internet can simply go to the Google search engine, type in the name of their senator or congressional representative along with the words "gun control" and be referred to the OnTheIssues.org website and that individual politician's voting record on gun issues. At the bottom of the specific web page at which you are looking, you will frequently find a reference to how these individuals are graded by the National Rifle Association. Pro-gun Kansas Republican Todd Tiahrt gets an "A" grade. Democrat House Speaker Nancy Pelosi earned an "F."

Vocally pro-gun Democrats who really do understand the importance of firearms in America are tragically few and far between. Sadly, for the relative handful of like-minded Democrats who have tried to lead the party away from the front lines of gun control hysteria, their party has been taken over by what many conservative critics call the "Nanny Statists," people who believe they are far better capable of making decisions for all of the people than the people, themselves.

The problem so upset former Georgia Democrat Governor and then Senator Zell Miller that he authored a book blasting the Democrats titled *A National Party No More: The Conscience of a Conservative Democrat*. How pro-gun can a "Zell Miller Democrat" be? Miller was elected to the board of directors of the National Rifle Association. You would hardly expect to see Barack Obama's name on that roster.

Miller hails from rural Georgia and has a deep-rooted connection with rural America. Obama, on the other hand, clearly has no connection to anything more rural than suburban Chicago, and – like far too many of his Democrat colleagues – appears to look upon rural, blue collar, gun-owning, church-going Americans as backwards bumpkins.

This condescending, elitist attitude leaped into the headlines in mid-April 2008 on the presidential campaign trail when Obama, appearing at an exclusive, private fundraiser in San Francisco, had this to say about rural Pennsylvanians: "You go into some of these small towns in Pennsylvania, and like a lot of small towns in the Midwest, the jobs have been gone now for 25 years and nothing's replaced them. And they fell through the Clinton administration, and the Bush administration, and each successive administration has said that somehow these communities are gonna regenerate and they have not. So it's not surprising then that they get bitter, they cling to guns or religion or antipathy to people who aren't like them or anti-immigrant sentiment or anti-trade sentiment as a way to explain their frustrations."

So, in the course of a single paragraph that streaked across the Internet gun rights forums like a California brushfire, Barack Obama perhaps best presented the image of what too many Americans quietly suspect is the dark side of the Democrat hierarchy, and how it looks down its nose at the values of average citizens, the so-called "middle America" that lies between the liberal East Coast and the liberal Left Coast. Translation: These rural "middle American redneck hicks" are bitter about immigrants, or minorities, so they clutch their guns and bibles to justify their hatred.

Whether this applies to every leading Democrat doesn't matter. It is what conservative Americans have come to believe is the norm for higher-ups in the party, and particularly for the party's dominant Far Left Wing, so essentially the stereotype becomes the reality, and it is reinforced every time Obama or someone like him makes such candidly foolish and insensitive remarks. And for gun owners, this explains at least in part why Democrats have emerged as the party of gun control.

That someone like Obama could, in such a short time from his first run for public office in the Illinois Legislature in the mid-1990s to midway through his first term as a United States senator, climb to the position of presidential aspirant simply reinforces the party's anti-gun image.

After all, Obama once sat on the board of the anti-gun Joyce Foundation, and according to a report on the Politico, during his time on that board the foundation issued "at least nine grants totaling nearly $2.7 million to groups" that support gun control. Further, the Politico reported, "The foundation funded legal scholarship advancing the theory that the Second Amendment does not protect individual gun owners' rights, as well as two groups that advocated handgun bans. And it paid to support a book called Every Handgun Is Aimed at You: The Case for Banning Handguns."

Also while he served on the Joyce Foundation board, a term which began in 1994 when he was 32 years old, Obama was paid $70,000 in directors fees. Despite claims to the contrary by his campaign, gun rights activists say this is damning evidence that Obama is and always has been a true believer in extremist gun control policies that the Joyce Foundation supports.

Incredibly, an organization billing itself as a pro-hunting, pro-gun alternative to the National Rifle Association – the American Hunters and Shooters Association (AHSA) – endorsed Barack Obama for president in the spring of 2008. AHSA's founders happen to be Democrats and its president, Ray Schoenke, ran for the Maryland governorship as a Democrat and he has been a major contributor to Democrat politicians, as well as having given money to the Brady Campaign to prevent Gun Violence.

Virtually every piece of virulent anti-gun rights legislation to be proposed and passed by Congress over the past generation was sponsored and championed by Democrats. It was gun control legislation pushed by Democrats in 1993 and 1994 that brought firearms owners to the polls en masse in November 1994 to unseat more than 50 members of Congress including then-Speaker of the House Tom Foley (the first time in 130 years that a House Speaker had been thrown out by his constituents) and take Congress away from the Bill Clinton Administration.

Despite claims to the contrary, Democrat party leaders, who seem to gravitate farther to the Left with every election cycle, have given American gun owners no solid proof that they stand behind their new-found loyalty to firearm civil rights.

When the nation is told by perennial anti-gunner Charles Schumer of New York – then a member of the U.S. House of Representatives and now the state's senior United States Senator – that, "We're here to tell the NRA their nightmare is true! We're going to hammer guns on ... We're going to beat guns into submission," American gun owners take note of the extremism that was unmasked in his gloating.

And they remember; Schumer has since insisted he "supports" the Second Amendment, during the 2006 election cycle when he was desperately recruiting fresh Democrats to run against Republicans, and trying to convince voters that Democrats are actually pro-gun rights. But gun owners will never forget this man's conduct, and they quite rightly consider his gun-grabbing sentiments to be shared by his ranking Democrat colleagues.

Those sentiments are certainly shared by California Sen. Dianne Feinstein, a San Francisco Democrat who helped Schumer spearhead the 1993-94 effort that led to the ten-year "ban" on so-called "assault weapons" that were in reality semiautomatic sport-utility rifles that look like military firearms.

But that was the problem: they merely "looked like" those military weapons, but in reality they weren't.

Feinstein wields considerable power due to her longevity on Capitol Hill, and she hates guns. Among gun rights activists, she exemplifies the credibility problem Democrats have within the firearms community. So long as she and others like her are around, and able to exert influence and power over the party's direction, Democrats will never enjoy the trust of gun owners.

How can Democrats claim to support gun rights without first essentially muzzling someone like Feinstein and repudiating the ideals she represents? Gun owners haven't forgotten Feinstein's February 5, 1995 performance on 60 Minutes, the CBS television "news magazine" during which she stated, about semi-auto rifles, "If I could have gotten 51 votes in the Senate of the United States for an outright ban, picking up every one of them…Mr. and Mrs. America, turn 'em all in, I would have done it. I could not do that. The votes weren't there."

Gun owners also remember that Feinstein proposed a measure under which all handgun and sport utility rifle owners would have to be licensed by the federal government. She claimed this was a plan that would keep handguns and semi-auto rifles out of the hands of criminals and people adjudicated as mentally incapacitated.

These gun licenses would initially cost $25 and be renewable on a five-year cycle. They could also be revoked.

From that moment forward, gun owners understood that Feinstein and other prominent Democrats who supported the measure had arbitrarily reached the conclusion that the Second Amendment right to keep and bear arms was nothing more than a privilege they could revoke at any time, and they were outraged.

Likewise, Feinstein and fellow Democrats voted against legislation that prevents federal funds from being used to confiscate privately-owned, legal firearms from law-abiding gun owners in the wake of a natural or man-made disaster. Gun owners saw that vote as an acknowledgement by Democrats that they support the warrantless seizure of firearms, without probable cause or due process.

Fellow California Democrat Senator Barbara Boxer does not fare any better, though she is somewhat less vociferous about her opposition to gun rights. But that hasn't stopped Boxer from being a firm supporter of renewing the ban on sport-utility rifles, and she voted for the original ban in 1994. She also supports a ban on so-called "cop killer bullets" even though experts have advised Congress that such legislation would essentially ban every bullet used in every centerfire hunting rifle in America.

Feinstein and Boxer joined Hillary Clinton and other prominent Democrats in voting against legislation that prohibits harassment lawsuits against firearms manufacturers. The majority of such lawsuits have ultimately been thrown out of court.

And then there's always New Jersey's inveterate anti-gun Democrat Frank Lautenberg, who retired from the Senate in 2000 only to be induced to run again by the Garden State's Democrat party machine in 2002 as a stand-in for Robert Torricelli, who withdrew from the race when a scandal erupted over illegal campaign contributions made by Korean-American businessman David Chang.

Torricelli, nicknamed "Torch," has since become a successful Democratic Party fund raiser and a partner in a New Jersey real estate development firm.

It was Lautenberg who, in 2003, introduced legislation along with then-Sen. Jon Corzine (D-NJ), and their anti-gun Democrat colleagues Edward M. Kennedy of Massachusetts and Jack Reed of Rhode Island, that would have essentially frozen the National Instant Check System and prevented law-abiding citizens from purchasing firearms. Under Lautenberg's plan, anytime that the Homeland Security threat level were to rise to the "Elevated" stage or higher, the NICS background check 72-hour maximum delay could be extended indefinitely. This was pandered as a move to block terrorists from buying guns during a state of emergency.

What Lautenberg and his fellow Democrats conveniently forgot to mention was the fact that ever since the September 11, 2001 terrorist attack, the Homeland Security threat level has always been "Elevated" or higher. They were hoping to sneak that by the public and their fellow lawmakers, thus enabling law enforcement agencies to effectively suspend all gun sales on the grounds of not being able to complete background checks.

Marching in lockstep

Gun rights activists sarcastically wonder whether it is something Democrats drink that causes them to climb aboard the Gun Control Express. Sometimes it appears they react with a knee jerk and propose, or support, any new gun control initiative that hits their desk. At other times, it is obvious to gun owners that they are following an agenda that does not favor the civil rights of people who own firearms.

A look at the voting records of Democrats John Kerry, Edward M. Kennedy,

Christopher Dodd, Joseph Biden, Carl Levin, Patty Murray, Dick Durbin and other leading Democrats and one quickly discerns that there is not a single restriction on the right to keep and bear arms that these individuals would not support. They are as predictable as the sunrise when it comes to their philosophy about private firearms ownership.

One cannot argue that this philosophy does not permeate the party from the top to the lower ranks.

For example, as this book was being written, the authors learned that New York State Senator Eric Adams, a Brooklyn Democrat representing the 20th Legislative district, had introduced legislation to require all Empire State gun owners to register all of their firearms at a cost of $15 each. This registration would be renewed annually at a cost of $10 per gun, and while it amounts to a hidden tax on gun owners to help bail out New York's budget, it is first and foremost a gun registration scheme in a state that already requires gun owners to have permits, and its architect is a Democrat.

Washington, D.C.'s Democrat Mayor Adrian Fenty is a devout anti-gunner, so devoted to disarming the citizens in his city that he carried the challenge to the District of Columbia handgun ban all the way to the United States Supreme Court.

New Orleans Mayor Ray Nagin is a hardcore Democrat, and it was under his administration that the post-Hurricane Katrina citywide gun confiscation was ordered. That operation involved law enforcement officers from all over the country who were instructed, without legal authority and certainly without warrant or probable cause, to seize every gun in the city, even at gunpoint if necessary, following the hurricane in 2005. It was an effort that so outraged the country that the Second Amendment Foundation and National Rifle Association quickly moved to have the gun grab stopped by the federal court.

Philadelphia Mayor Michael Nutter reigns over one of the most violent and crime-ridden cities in the nation, and he is virulently anti-gun. In early 2008, he pushed for gun restrictions that ran counter to state preemption, and the National Rifle Association sped to court to obtain an injunction against their enforcement.

The package Nutter signed included a limit on the number of guns a person can buy in a calendar month, and a requirement that citizens report lost or stolen guns within 24 hours. He knew these ordinances ran afoul of a 1996 Pennsylvania Supreme Court decision that squarely upheld state preemption authority on all gun regulation, but being a stoic anti-gunner, he signed them anyway and announced they would be enforced.

Chicago Mayor Richard Daley is a Democrat demagogue, so driven by his dislike for guns that he constantly pressures the Illinois State Legislature to adopt his extremist gun policies statewide. He reins over a city where legal handguns have been banned for a generation, yet – like Washington, D.C.

– the homicide rate typically places the city among the top five or ten most murder-prone big cities in the nation.

And do not forget San Francisco's far Left Liberal Democrat Mayor Gavin Newsom, who presides over a city government so tilted to the extreme that they fought an acknowledged losing battle to ban handguns in order to make a political statement. That handgun ban was nullified by a lawsuit filed jointly by the Second Amendment Foundation and National Rifle Association, along with the Law Enforcement Alliance of America, California Association of Firearms Retailers and some San Francisco residents.

So this isn't just a Hillary Clinton problem or a Barack Obama problem, it is a party problem, and even though freshman Democrats may insist they are pro-gunners – and have the records to support that claim – their leadership consistently leans far in the opposite direction, regardless of the rhetoric.

While Democrat activists are quick to dismiss the oft-repeated sentiment, originally explained by late President Ronald Reagan when he first became involved in California politics in the 1960s that "I didn't leave the Democratic Party, the party left me," the truth clearly was on Reagan's side. Millions of gun owners whose parents had supported the Democratic Party, and who probably cast their first ballots for Democrat politicians, are now solid Republicans or Libertarians.

Guess whose fault that is?

Once the Far Left seized control of the Democratic Party in the late 1960s and 1970s, their first target was guns. The 1968 Gun Control Act was passed in the wake of two horrible assassinations in the spring of that year that claimed the lives of two liberal icons, Dr. Martin Luther King and Senator Robert F. Kennedy. The Left seemed to hold the firearms responsible, as they did with the November 1963 slaying of President John F. Kennedy, the senator's older brother, rather than the assassins, and it has been that way ever since.

When San Francisco Democrat Mayor George Moscone and businessman Harvey Milk were gunned down inside city hall by City Supervisor Dan White, Moscone's successor, Dianne Feinstein, went on a rampage against guns. It was under her administration that the city passed a gun ban that was immediately challenged by the Second Amendment Foundation in court as a violation of state preemption, and the Foundation won that lawsuit. As mentioned earlier, Feinstein has gone on to become one of the United States Senate's most virulent gun control extremists.

It is that extremism which alienates gun owners, because they are convinced that regardless what Democratic politicians may say about supporting their right to own a gun, it is how they vote on issues affecting gun ownership that really counts. In that respect, as a party, Democrats have spent the past 40 years generating bad will among gun owners.

It may be confusing to some, and amusing to others, but despite their track record, Democrats continue attempting to sell themselves as pro-gun candidates while their records belie everything they say. And that brings us around to Senator Barack Hussein Obama.

'I didn't see it'

In 1996, when Barack Obama was essentially a "nobody" running for his first political office in Illinois, he was sent a questionnaire from a liberal nonprofit group based in Chicago that asked candidates about their stands on such issues as the death penalty, health issues, energy, the environment, and gun control.

The responses on that questionnaire may never have surfaced with such a significant impact if Obama had not, just 12 years later, skyrocketed to the national spotlight as a front-running candidate for the Democratic Party's nomination to run for president.

On that questionnaire, candidate Obama's positions were spelled out succinctly: He opposes capital punishment and mandatory sentencing, he is against prosecuting juveniles as adults for serious crimes, he supports a ban on the manufacture, sale and possession of handguns and semi-automatic rifles, and he backs mandatory waiting periods for firearms purchases.

These are not the positions of a man who, years later, would profess to support the Second Amendment as an individual civil right. And Obama even tried to distance himself from the questionnaire when it eventually surfaced, claiming that the answers were provided by an aide.

But then Kenneth P. Vogel, writing on the March 31, 2008 Politico.com website, revealed that Obama had "actually (been) interviewed" by the nonprofit group that issued the questionnaire. Furthermore, Vogel reported, Obama's handwriting appears on the original document, which was an "amended version" of the questionnaire.

A dozen years later, and running a dazzling campaign for the presidential nomination, Obama's campaign staff adamantly denied that their candidate ever held such views. His fact sheet as a presidential candidate asserts that Obama "has consistently supported common-sense gun control, as well as the rights of law-abiding gun owners."

Let's go back in history. Barack Obama, according to official and unofficial biographies, was born August 4, 1961 to a Kenyan father and American mother. His early life was spent primarily in Hawaii and in Jakarta, Indonesia, with his mother and Indonesian stepfather.

Obama graduated from Columbia University in 1983 and moved to Chicago two years later where he worked for a church-based organization helping in poor neighborhoods. He went on to Harvard Law School, graduating in 1991 and the following year, he married the former Michelle Robinson. The couple has two daughters.

He worked as a community organizer, civil rights attorney and gave university lectures and then ran successfully for a seat in the Illinois Senate, where he served from 1997 to 2004. He was unable to win a 2000 election to the U.S. House of Representatives, but three years later, he launched a successful bid to become the junior senator from Illinois.

With a political life firmly entrenched in Chicago politics, Barack Obama has undoubtedly formed his opinions about firearms from the perspective of the anti-gun Chicago political machine. And while those positions may hold him in good stead with the Democratic Party hierarchy, they are not well-received by the firearms community.

Obama really angered the gun rights community about ten days before his foolish remarks about rural Pennsylvanians, when he told a Pennsylvania newspaper that he did not approve of concealed carry.

He was quoted by the *Pittsburgh Tribune-Review* in its April 2, 2008 edition stating, "I am not in favor of concealed weapons. I think that creates a potential atmosphere where more innocent people could (get shot during) altercations."

Reaction from gun owners was swift and blistering, and best represented by the demand from the Citizens Committee for the Right to Keep and Bear Arms (CCRKBA) – a national grassroots organization based in Bellevue, Washington – that Obama apologize to gun-carrying citizens for what they considered an insult. Call it political theatrics on the part of the CCRKBA, but the demand hit a nerve with gun owners who were livid over Obama's inference that they posed some sort of public threat.

CCRKBA noted that legally-licensed and permitted citizens have gone through background checks and, in many states, required training courses in order to secure their right to carry a concealed handgun. The group suggested that Obama had confused "legally-armed, law-abiding Americans with inner-city thugs, gang-bangers and other criminals who carry guns illegally." Naturally, in Illinois where Obama cut his political teeth and rose up through the ranks, he did not grow up in an environment where citizens carry guns because Illinois has no "right to keep and bear arms" provision in its state constitution. Further, Chicago – where Obama sank his roots – and several surrounding suburban communities have virtually banned handguns, so the only people carrying handguns are either cops or criminals.

It comes as a shock to people like Obama and many other pro-gun control Democrats, that state-issued licenses and permits in 48 states are for concealed carry. In many, if not the majority of states, the practice of open carry – that is, carrying a holstered handgun on one's belt – is perfectly legal, which is easy to determine if one does a little research on individual state firearm statutes. Indeed, over the past couple of years, something of a sub-movement within the firearms community has sprang up promoting open carry. Its proponents note that simply because the practice has fallen out of vogue does not make it illegal.

That said, if Barack Obama and other Democrats have heartburn over concealed carry, they may have coronaries if they spend enough time in places like Vermont, Alaska, Ohio, Washington, Montana, Idaho, Oregon and Arizona for example. Those are states where the open carry movement appears to be strongest.

In the early 1990s, former Washington Gov. Mike Lowry, a one-term liberal anti-gun Democrat whose political career went through something of a political meltdown over a sexual harassment problem, pushed through a statute that banned open carry in the Evergreen State. That statute was repealed almost immediately after Lowry left office under pressure from county prosecutors who told state lawmakers that the statute was unenforceable.

Why The Brand Sticks

Perhaps the headline said it all on February 25, 2004 when Newsmax. com the Internet news service, picked up a story from the Associated Press about a new series of gun control initiatives in Congress. The headline: "Senate Democrats Push Anti-gun Measures."

Gun owners see that sort of headline often enough to convince them that as a party, Democrats are like the leopard that cannot change its spots, regardless how hard the party or individual candidates try. It is always Democrats who are pushing anti-gun measures, and try as they might to shed the image by changing their rhetoric, as they did in preparation for the 2006 mid-term elections, it is only a matter of time before they collectively return to the gun control pattern.

On December 17, 2005, the Boston Globe reported, "The Democratic Party, long identified with gun control, is rethinking its approach to the gun debate, seeking to improve the chances of its candidates in Western states where hunters have been wary of casting votes for a party with a national reputation of being against guns.

"The Democrats' effort to soften their rhetoric on gun control is similar to the party's recent efforts to recast its message on abortion, maintaining their support of abortion rights but welcoming more Democrats who favor restrictions on the procedure."

Notice how this report was worded. Democrats were softening their rhetoric, but there is nothing in there about rejecting or repudiating their long-standing history of gun control efforts. What this tells gun owners is that Democrats not only cling to their gun control agenda, they also still believe their own erroneous stereotype of the average gun owner: A rather stupid redneck who might easily be duped by a change in rhetoric.

In that same Boston Globe report, Paul Hackett, at the time a candidate for the U.S. Senate in Ohio, told a reporter, "As a party, our lack of understanding of gun sports is hurting us."

While Hackett was sending a signal to his party leaders, the signal those same leaders sent to gun owner constituents was much more defining about how the party still operates.

On February 14, 2006, the New York Times told the story about Hackett, and his departure from politics, by noting that the Iraq war veteran, a member of the National Rifle Association and former Marine had been rather unceremoniously urged to get out of the race against Republican Mike DeWine by the same party leaders – New York Sen. Charles Schumer and Nevada Sen. Harry Reid – who had recruited him to run in the first place. Instead, the party decided it wanted Rep. Sherrod Brown to run against DeWine.

Brown has an anti-gun voting record in Congress and earned an "F" rating from the NRA. He won the election, but it was something of a shoo-in because DeWine had such a liberal voting record, including against gun rights, that his constituents simply abandoned him. The election found DeWine trounced by Brown, who garnered better than 55 percent of the popular vote. DeWine could not even pull 45 percent of the vote.

Democrat leaders had tried to throw Hackett a "consolation prize" of sorts by encouraging him to run for the House of Representatives, but he rejected that outright. He had given his word to three other Democrats that he would not enter that particular race, and unlike Schumer and Reid, former Marine Paul Hackett kept his word.

Perhaps it was Hackett's honesty that doomed his campaign. After all, he had been quoted in the Boston Globe noting that candidates who rejected gun control "are depicted by some in our party as a bunch of yahoos, and we're not. We are just good Democrats who are pro-gun."

Instead of becoming a rising star in the party, Hackett was betrayed, according to the New York Times account, in favor of a perennial anti-gunner, and the way it happened was rather heartless and cold. Hackett told the Times that he had learned Democrat party leaders had been calling his donors and asking that they stop contributing to his campaign.

Hackett, who was vocally outspoken against the Iraq war in which he had served, had this to say in summation: "For me, this is a second betrayal. First, my government misused and mismanaged the military in Iraq, and now my own party is afraid to support candidates like me."

But the betrayal goes beyond Paul Hackett. It was essentially a betrayal of gun owners by first recruiting a pro-gun Democrat and then throwing him out. Gun owners in Ohio watched it happen and were disgusted.

In a situation like this, there is nothing to keep in perspective, as career politicians and political gamesmen are often given to observing. Democrats had a popular, straight-talking, pro-gun military veteran who arguably might have defeated DeWine ever worse than he was, but the Democrats tossed him aside for a seven-term Congressional anti-gun insider with whom they felt more comfortable.

Perhaps the Boston Globe story from December 2005 explained the problem as gun owners perceive it, noting "some…party leaders acknowledge that as a group, Democrats still have an anti-gun image that could hinder even those candidates who oppose gun control. Some of the party's most prominent members -- including Senator Edward M. Kennedy of Massachusetts and House minority leader Nancy Pelosi of California -- support gun control, a more common view among lawmakers from urban areas."

One might also observe that it is "a more common view among lawmakers whose names are followed by a 'D'," identifying them as a Democrat.

Three

'THERE ARE TOO MANY GUNS...'

Campaigning against the firearm civil rights of every American citizen – and not just this nation's estimated 80 million gun owners; after all, a constitutionally-protected, fundamental civil right belongs to all citizens, not just those who exercise it – has become an obsession with *The New York Times*.

So, when a champion of gun control emerges to take on the "evil gun lobby," this "newspaper of record" is quick to lionize that individual. In the case of Hillary Diane Rodham Clinton, former First Lady, junior United States senator from New York and a candidate for the 2008 Democratic party presidential nomination, the *New York Times* didn't simply support her efforts, it adored and adorned her with favorable news coverage, the kind of publicity that money can't buy for a cause that the *New York Times* has appointed itself to promote to the proverbial bitter end.

There can be no doubt that, regardless whether Hillary were to become president of the United States or remain in the U.S. Senate, *The New York Times* would continue to fawn over her every effort to ratchet down on the firearms rights of every American citizen.

Of course, the *Times* is free to editorialize as it sees fit. That is, after all, within the realm of press freedom and fair comment, protected by the First Amendment. But somewhere in the course of striving for its lofty goal of being one of the nation's premier newspapers, the *New York Times* lost sight of the fact that the Bill of Rights, that great document authored by a bunch of "old dead white guys" as the late Charlton Heston, former President of the National Rifle Association, was fond of calling them, is an all-or-nothing package.

One cannot cherry pick from among the rights affirmed and protected by the Bill of Rights, and leave those with which you do not agree by the wayside of history. You either believe in and defend as strenuously the right to keep

27

and bear arms as you do the rights of free speech, press and religion, the right to be secure in your own home, and the right against self-incrimination, or the entire document is essentially worthless.

That is because if today you whimsically dismiss the right secured under the Second Amendment, in the interest of political correctness, then what civil right would you willingly abandon tomorrow?

This is a question that no politician has dared to address head-on, but it appears that in the case of Hillary Clinton, her actions speak louder than any patronizing words ever could. She has been "acting" out her true feelings about gun rights for many years, and more actively since she was elected to the United States Senate in 2000.

In a May 9, 1999 article about First Lady Hillary Clinton's emergency as "point person" for her husband's administration on the gun control issue, *New York Times* reporter Katharine Q. Seelye made it abundantly clear in her lead paragraph: "Stepping up the Clinton Administration's campaign against gun violence, Hillary Rodham Clinton used an emotional White House ceremony today to call on Americans to press Congress to 'buck the gun lobby' and pass several gun control measures."

This was less than a month after the Columbine High School massacre in Littleton, Colorado – an event that brought gun control organizations literally out of the woodwork to exploit in an effort to advance their anti-gun rights agenda – and Hillary Clinton was out front and in top form.

Of course, the Times story unintentionally identified the cornerstone of the extremist gun control movement, emotionalism. The gun control lobby certainly doesn't have much fact on its side.

Take, for example, the gun control lobby's inflammatory campaign against right-to-carry statutes passed over the past several years in dozens of states. Invariably, anti-gun activists and professional gun control proponents have trooped to state legislatures and editorial board meetings at all-too-sympathetic newspapers to predict such laws would result in "Wild West shoot-outs" and "OK Corral" confrontations over minor traffic mishaps. They claimed children and police officers would be placed at greater risk, and that gunshot deaths and injuries would soar.

There has been but one problem with these claims. They're all bullshit. Don't care for the word? Then perhaps Hillary and the *New York Times*, and several other "newspapers of record" should stop shoveling it under the guise of news or "fair" comment on the editorial pages.

It is somewhat rare for the press to carefully examine the results of concealed carry reform, but when such reports are published, those who initially spread the hysteria are typically silent or very subdued, as data demonstrates such laws work. That was the experience reported on January 6, 2008 by the *Detroit Free Press* in which reporter Dawson Bell revealed that after six years of expanded concealed carry in Michigan, "the incidence of violent crime...has been, on average, below the rate of the previous six years. The overall incidence of death from firearms, including suicide and accidents, has also declined."

The newspaper said 155,000 Michigan residents, about one in every 65 citizens, is now licensed to carry. That figure is up dramatically from the approximately 25,000 who were licensed prior to passage of the right-to-carry law in 2001, and it is telling. Where newspapers and gun control proponents had argued that the law was being changed only to satisfy the desires of a very small minority of Michiganders, it turned out that tens of thousands of Great Lakes State residents wanted carry permits but had never before had the opportunity to obtain them without interference from local authorities.

The newspaper quoted Woodhaven Police Chief Michael Martin, co-chair of the legislative committee for the Michigan Association of Chiefs of Police. His observation: "I think the general consensus out there from law enforcement is that things were not as bad as we expected."

Even one of the state's concealed carry critics, Dr. Kenneth Levin of West Bloomfield, had changed his tune, but with the reservations of an avowed anti-gunner who simply cannot bring himself to admit he was mistaken. In 2001, the newspaper recalled, he had written a letter to the editor predicting an "inevitable first victim of road or workplace rage as a result of this law."

Now, however, he was somewhat muted, while still in begrudging denial that his earlier rant was in error: "It probably hasn't turned out as bad as I thought. I don't think I was wrong, but my worst fears weren't realized."

A Bellevue, Washington-based grassroots gun rights organization, the Citizens Committee for the Right to Keep and Bear Arms, pounced on the Free Press report, issuing a statement that harshly criticized gun control fanaticism and the media's willingness to believe the rhetoric years earlier.

"Lawful concealed carry reduces crime and does not result in mass mayhem as the anti-self-defense crowd wanted us believe," the organization stated. "Six years ago, they pulled out all the stops, fabricated every dire prediction they could imagine, and essentially told lies about concealed carry and passed them off as truth, and too many in the media ate it up as if it were manna from Heaven."

Mark A. Taff, then-CCRKBA executive director, put it bluntly: "Anti-gun rights extremists established a track record for prevarication in state after state where they rabidly fought right-to-carry statutes, and in case after case, including Michigan, every one of their claims has been statistically refuted."

Don't confuse Hillary with facts

When then-First Lady Hillary Rodham Clinton spoke to the National Education Association in Orlando, Florida on July 5, 1999, she left little

29

doubt with one of the nation's most liberal lobbying groups where she stands on the issue of firearms ownership, and how that issue should be framed.

As noted in the previous chapter, she said that "there are too many guns and too many children have access to those guns-and we have to act to prevent that."

But that year, according to statistics from the National Safety Council, quoted by the University of Michigan Health Systems, a total of 73 children under age 5 died in a firearm-related mishap, and 416 youngsters ages 5-14 died from gunshot wounds. Granted, 489 accidental or intentional fatal child shootings is tragic, but one thing it is not is an epidemic, yet gun control proponents will portray this as an epidemic.

They get away with that by adding all the gunshot deaths for teenagers ages 15-19 years, calling them "children" and overlooking the fact that in a large percentage of those cases, the victims and the killers were gang members or gang "wannabes" involved in some illegal activity, such as drug dealing, and they died in turf wars.

Other teens in this age group committed suicide and some were the victims of genuine accidents.

Various sources will confirm that firearms accidents among children have declined steadily over the past quarter-century, despite increases in gun ownership.

More youngsters die accidentally in drownings, car crashes and even choking on their own food than die from gunshot wounds according to the National Safety Council.

This information is certainly available to the First Lady, and to a U.S. Senator, yet when she was on the campaign trail in 1999 and 2000, Hillary Clinton didn't discuss water safety and the importance of wearing a personal flotation device (PFD), nor did she launch a tirade about child safety seats or the use of seatbelts. She went after firearms as the menace to child safety.

In the May 1999 *New York Times* article, Hillary discussed then-pending gun control legislation at the White House event, stating that members of the Senate "need to hear from all of us."

"Give them the encouragement," she said, "to do what they know is right and to remind them that there are many, many millions of American voters who will stand behind political leaders who are brave enough to buck the gun lobby, wherever that may take us, so that they will vote for the measures that we know will save lives."

And what measures was she talking about? Raising the age limit for handgun possession – with some exemptions – to 21 years, closing the so-called "gun show loophole" by requiring background checks on private transactions (now exempt under the Brady Law, which Bill Clinton signed in 1993), prosecution of parents if they "recklessly or negligently" allow their child to access a firearm and subsequently commit a crime with that gun, and expansion of the federal government's gun tracing program.

The lines have shifted on some of those proposals, with Hillary Clinton always on the side of increased regulation and restriction.

For example, she voted against a measure that protects sensitive trace data, administered by the federal Bureau of Alcohol, Tobacco, Firearms and Explosives, from misuse by anti-gun big city mayors who would use that to mouth harassment lawsuits against firearms dealers and gun makers.

And in May of 2000, when she was campaigning hard for that U.S. Senate seat in New York, once again it was the *New York Times* that gave her a forum.

As reported in the May 10 edition by writer Adam Nagourney, Hillary Clinton "endorsed a series of stringent gun-control measures." Those proposals included "licensing of all new gun owners and the registration of new guns." She also threw her support behind creation of a "ballistic fingerprint" database, proposed by then-Gov. George Pataki, an anti-gun Republican, yet at the time – and even today – there remains ample evidence that such technology doesn't work, and everyone knows it.

It was in that story where Mrs. Clinton was also quoted as stating, "'Many will argue that we don't need sensible gun control, and that these measures undermine the rights of gun owners. And of course, we all know the slogan that guns don't kill, only people do. We have to do more to stand up to those who refuse to believe the reality that guns do kill, and that common-sense gun measures can make a difference."

She used the opportunity to remind the newspaper and its readers that she would be attending the "Million Mom March" on Mother's Day, where she would be rubbing elbows with other anti-gunners who had organized that numerically-challenged anti-gun organization.

What was interesting about that particular *Times* piece was that it revealed her to have been more out-front on gun control than her husband, who has been portrayed by NRA's Wayne LaPierre as "the most anti-gun president in the history of this country." That would, it appears, have to be revised if Hillary Clinton were to attain the presidency, as her forcefulness on the issue seems considerably more robust than that of her husband's.

When Bill Clinton had spoken at a fund-raiser the previous Friday evening, the newspaper noted, he had seemed almost conciliatory about pending gun control legislation: "I hope we can avoid yet another big fight in Washington between the N.R.A. and others."

Yet, on May 9, 2000, according to a report by CNN, there was First Lady Hillary speaking to the Newspaper Association of America in New York City, delivering that remark quoted above by the *New York Times* issue of the following day, leaving one to wonder whether the "two-for-the-price-of-one" team was playing "Good Cop/Bad Cop" to American gun owners.

In the process of attacking the firearms issue, Hillary overlooked the fact that the gun industry is one of the most highly-regulated industries in the nation.

"It doesn't make much sense that we regulate toy guns but not real guns," CNN quoted her as stating.

But then again, Hillary was using rhetoric that had been used repeatedly by anti-gunners who have long falsely asserted that the making of teddy bears is more regulated than the making of firearms. Good for a sound bite, perhaps, but demonstrably false.

Hillary Clinton is no fan of the firearms industry, and vice versa, since she voted against legislation that protects gun makers from frivolous harassment lawsuits filed by anti-gun mayors. Despite her opposition in 2004 and again in 2005, Congress passed the Protection of Lawful Commerce in Arms Act.

For all the hoopla generated by passage of the Brady Law in 1993 during Bill Clinton's first term – a major reason why gun owners descended on the polls in 1994 and changed the face of Congress for the first time in 40 years – there is very little evidence that background checks, a key ingredient of the legislation that set up the National Instant Check System (NICS), have prevented a single violent crime.

Indeed, Hillary Clinton acknowledged as much during the South Carolina Democratic presidential primary debate, broadcast on MSNBC on April 26, 2007. Asked whether the federal government had failed to prevent the Virginia Tech massacre just seven days before that debate, she responded, "We now know that the background check system didn't work, because certainly this shooter, as he's called, had been involuntarily committed as a threat to himself and others. And, yet, he could walk in and buy a gun."

But according to the website FactCheck.com, that's not true. Explaining that Hillary "slipped up in her description of the Virginia Tech killings," the website said that she overstated the handling of killer Seung-Hui Cho by a Virginia court in 2005. Here's how FactCheck.org described the situation:

"It's correct that Seung-Hui Cho had a court-documented history of mental illness that should have precluded his purchase of a firearm. And he was indeed found to present 'an imminent danger to himself as a result of mental illness' in a ruling dated December 14, 2005. But the Judge did not check a box that would have declared Cho 'an imminent danger to others.' Moreover, the judge declined to involuntarily commit Cho and sent him to outpatient counseling. Clinton's confusion on this might stem from bad reporting by some news outlets that said Cho was found to be a danger to himself and others."

Granted, at the time she made that statement, it had only been a week since the massacre, and not all of the facts had been completely sorted out. But it demonstrates the fact that the NICS background check, which the "two-for-the-price-of-one" Clinton Administration had championed in 1993 after gun rights organizations had forced the original legislation to be amended, eliminating a federal waiting period after NICS went on-line in November 1998, really didn't work here because Cho was never identified to the system as being disqualified.

Is that a NICS failure, or a failure of the Virginia courts? It was interesting that Hillary saw it as a NICS failure, while skillfully avoiding any discussion about how the background check system had been the cornerstone of her husband's Brady Law package.

Her acknowledgement that the NICS system had failed could be part of her overall strategy to "soften" her rhetoric on gun control, at least long enough to get the nomination, and what she believes to be her deserved election. Changing one's tune in the course of an election campaign, or doing anything in order to win, is nothing new for politicians, but according to the *Wall Street Journal* of January 23, 2008, in an opinion piece headlined "Obama's Clinton Education," Bill and Hillary Clinton have developed this sort of thing to an art form.

That editorial discussed the choreographed attacks on Senator Barack Obama by Bill Clinton while Hillary maintained at least the visage of remaining above the fray, a role reversal of the period during the Ken Starr investigation in which Hillary lamented on television about the "vast right wing conspiracy" that was set on ousting her rather untruthful husband.

But the editorial put the Clinton strategy in its proper perspective. In discussing Obama's rude awakening to the fact that Bill and Hillary Clinton are something of a political tag team, the WSJ observed, "The Illinois Senator is still a young man, but not so young as to have missed the 1990s. He nonetheless seems to be awakening slowly to what everyone else already knows about the Clintons, which is that they will say and do whatever they 'gotta' say or do to win."

Which brings us around to Hillary's insistence that she "supports the Second Amendment." Gun rights activists shake their heads and roll their eyes to the heavens when she makes such pronouncements. They join Internet discussions with such observations as "The Second Amendment doesn't need her support."

The firearms community is hardly convinced by Hillary Clinton's newfound affinity for the Second Amendment, considering that she has spent the past several years voting for every infringement that came to the Senate, and even before that, campaigning for tougher gun laws as First Lady. When she fought for renewal of the ban on so-called "assault weapons" it would have been impossible for her to not know that such a ban was marginal at best in reducing violent crime.

According to a report for the Department of Justice done by the Jerry Lee Center of Criminology at the University of Pennsylvania in June 2004 entitled *An Update Assessment of the Federal Assault Weapons Ban: Impacts on Gun Markets and Gun Violence,* authors Christopher S. Koper, Daniel J.

Woods and Jeffrey A. Roth noted, "(Assault weapons) were used in only a small fraction of gun crimes prior to the ban: about 2% according to most studies and no more than 8%."

But the ban was a symbolic victory for the "two-for-the-price-of-one" Clinton White House and Hillary, like anti-gun colleagues including Senators Dianne Feinstein, Charles Schumer and Edward M. Kennedy did not want to let it go. However, stubborn resistance to the facts does not your fantasy make into truth.

Professor John R. Lott, a veteran firearms crime researcher and author of books on gun control including *More Guns = Less Crime* and *The Bias Against Guns* revealed in a March 25, 2004 essay for *National Review Online* that "there is not a single academic study showing that either the state or federal bans have reduced violent crime. Even research funded by the Justice Department under the Clinton administration concluded merely that the bans 'impact on gun violence has been uncertain'."

Even though she is now declaring her "support" for the Second Amendment, there is no indication that Hillary has seriously backed off from stands that she has held over the years favoring licensing and registration. And she now has a record that belies any effort to convince American hunters, shooters and gun collectors or citizens who arm themselves merely for personal protection that she is anything but a gun control hard-liner masquerading as a moderate.

FOUR

'SMARTEST WOMAN' GETS AN 'F'

Gennifer Flowers. Monica Lewinsky. Paula Jones. Kathleen Willey. Juanita Broaddrick. They probably all wished they owned a gun.

The stories told by and about these women and their encounters with former President William Jefferson Clinton, whether given credibility or otherwise in at least a couple of cases, have left many of the disgraced ex-president's sharpest critics wondering how all of this could have happened essentially under the nose of the person who many people claim is the "smartest woman in the world," Hillary Diane Rodham Clinton.

The Lewinsky scandal was true and there was a stained blue dress to prove it. Bill Clinton eventually acknowledged his affair with Flowers, but only after a lengthy period of denial, same as he did with Lewinsky until that dress showed up. Everyone in the country recalls that well-rehearsed, finger-pointing statement of pained indignance: "I...did not have sexual relations with that woman, Miss Lewinsky."

Except that, by all definitions of "sexual relations" other than Bill Clinton's perhaps, he did. Several times. And he wasn't too tidy about it, either.

Through it all, Hillary has stuck by, or perhaps to, Bill Clinton and that has raised questions about whether she did it to take advantage of his proven ability to gather a crowd and raise cash, or because she realizes his faults and takes him, anyway.

During the early days of 2008 when the campaign between Hillary and Senator Barack Obama heated up, pundits concluded that Hillary had kept Bill around in order to be the bare knuckles advocate and defender of his polarizing and ambitious wife. The former president took a considerable amount of heat for that, even from his own party faithful, yet he stayed on the campaign trail, defending or denying his remarks as he apparently felt necessary, at times even to his wife's chagrin.

Columnist Peggy Noonan, writing in the *Wall Street Journal* January 25, 2008, made note of the political discomfort Bill Clinton was causing in his own party. Noonan quoted writer William Greider's remarks in *The Nation*, in which he unabashedly said that both Bill and Hillary Clinton are "smarmily duplicitous underneath, meanwhile jabbing hard at the groin area. They are a slippery pair and come as a package. The nation is at fair risk of getting them back in the White House for four years."

Yet there was an aspect of this flap, an angle that everyone seemed to overlook, at least publicly: How did this primary season performance by the Clintons reflect on Hillary's true capability of serving as president, to say nothing of the Clintons' double-teaming a black man who was at least as viable a candidate as Hillary (and certainly proved it with a string of primary victories that sent her campaign reeling)?

After all, one could have easily reasoned at the time, "If Hillary needed to depend on her husband to do the heavy work, the dirty work, during her campaign, what happens to President Hillary in a real crisis situation? Does she defer to her lothario Bubba – if he's not too busy staining somebody's dress – to go head-to-head with, say, Osama Bin Laden or Mahmoud Ahmadinejad? Will she be able to make the tough decisions, or will she turn that over to Bill who, after all, would not be president and would have been elected by nobody in 2008?

Then, again, a President Hillary might have just reminded the nation that they got "two-for-the-price-of-one." History is always the judge of such things, and history is not known for its leniency.

In the meantime, America's 80 million-plus firearms owners can judge for themselves whether Hillary Clinton's own repeated proclamations about supporting the Second Amendment are worth more than a counterfeit coin. Or maybe they will simply take a signal from gun rights organizations, specifically the National Rifle Association and Gun Owners of America, both of which have given "the smartest woman in the world" an "F" grade on gun rights, and continue to act accordingly so long as Hillary remains in public office.

GOA spells it out on its official website: "There is really little point in detailing (Hillary) Clinton's vote-by-vote record on the Second Amendment. That's because every single time there has been a gun-related vote in the Senate that GOA has tracked, Sen. Clinton has voted anti-gun. Without fail, she opts to restrict the rights of Americans to keep and bear firearms -- 100% of the time."

However, GOA does detail her record and from the perspective of a gun rights organization, she has been a disaster.

Beginning in the 107th Congress, her freshman term, Senator Hillary Diane Rodham Clinton of New York voted in support of S. 924, a bill expanding federal police power in "firearms-related incidents." She supported legislation to ban gun shows, another bill to register gun buyers for 90 days, a bill creating a lifetime ban on gun ownership by juvenile offenders, and a measure to audit background check information, making it available for both criminal and civil inquiries, GOA'S website recalls.

During the 108th Congress, Hillary supported a ten-year extension of the ban on so-called "assault weapons." She also supported a measure to create a national "ballistic imaging" registry of all new firearms, and a bill that would have expanded the powers of the Bureau of Alcohol, Tobacco, Firearms and Explosives.

During that same Congressional session, Hillary also backed a plan to have the Federal Bureau of Investigation keep records of gun sales to persons on so-called "watch lists," plus a bill to ban polymer-framed firearms, a bill that would have expanded and renewed the ban on "assault weapons," another bill that would have banned certain magazines for firearms, required trigger locks and restricted handgun purchases to one per month, according to GOA.

In the 109th Congress, Hillary supported a move to ban .50-caliber centerfire rifles, which have been demonized by the radical anti-gun Left. They have never been used to shoot down an airliner, as opponents have hysterically claimed they would be. Indeed, the authors could find only a handful of cases, less than a half-dozen, in which such rifles have ever actually or allegedly been fired during the course of a criminal act, and while even a few such crimes are too many, their use has been so rare that such incidents are virtually unheard of. It is not true, for example, that one was used to kill a Colorado police officer.

Fifty-caliber rifles have certainly been found in searches of other crime scenes and residences of criminal suspects, but it does not appear any of those guns had been fired. None of that matters to anti-gunners, Hillary included.

She also backed legislation that would have banned certain semiautomatic firearms, another measure to revive the semi-auto ban, a measure that would allow the FBI to keep records of gun sales to persons on "watch lists" for ten years, and a measure that would have, according to GOA, treated firearms offenses "as though they were Mafia or gang-related crimes."

Hillary twice voted against the Protection of Lawful Commerce in Arms Act, a law that passed despite her opposition. It protects gun makers from the kinds of junk lawsuits filed by municipal governments that try to hold the firearms industry responsible for violent crime committed by armed felons.

She joined 15 other senators in voting against the Vitter Amendment in 2006. That was the legislation that prohibits the use of federal funds for the confiscation of lawfully-held firearms in the aftermath of a natural or man-made disaster. This was the bill that sailed through Congress after the outrageous conduct of law enforcement officers, seizing firearms at gunpoint without warrant or probable cause, was revealed.

Hillary Clinton's anti-gun voting slowed down in the 110th Congress, however, perhaps because she was trying to soften her image – though hardly her position – on gun control, and also because she was so busy on the campaign trail that she was not available to vote. But she did find the time to support, once again, the legislation equating firearms offenses with gangland crimes, and another bill that expands federal funding, and control, of local law enforcement.

Yet, as the *New York Sun* editorialized on December 12, 2007, Hillary's campaign issued a rather oddball news release challenging the "electability" of Democrat rival Senator Barack Obama because he had supported the idea of banning all handguns.

"Well, it's a pleasure to welcome Mrs. Clinton to the Second Amendment side of the debate," the Sun's sarcasm-laced editorial stated. "It's a new development; back in 2000, when Mrs. Clinton was running for Senate, she backed the 'Million Mom March' for gun control…"

Such remarks, especially in the pages of a newspaper with such a wide readership as that of the *New York Sun*, reminded voters of Hillary Clinton's history regarding gun control, and such reminders certainly did not help her bid for the Democratic Party nomination.

The 'non-incumbent incumbent'

In a December 18, 2007 opinion piece in the *San Francisco Chronicle*, writer Debra J. Saunders poked quite a bit of her own sarcasm at the junior senator from New York when she took issue with Bill Clinton's remark about Barack Obama's lack of experience.

The same could have easily been said about Bill Clinton in 1992, Saunders observed.

"Neither Clinton saw much virtue in experience in 1991 – when the Arkansas governor was challenging the very experienced President George H.W. Bush. Now HRC (Hillary) is running as the experienced Democrat. She's the nonincumbent incumbent."

True enough, Hillary has said and suggested more than once on the campaign trail that she has "the experience." At being what? First Lady? Knowing where the White House restrooms are located? Or, more likely, being one of her husband's closest political advisors during his "two-for-the-price-of-one" presidency. Indeed, there are some people who believe Hillary managed Bill's defense strategy after the Lewinsky scandal broke, and she probably did have experience in that arena, considering that Bill Clinton seemed to be dogged by what his chief of staff in Arkansas, Betsey Wright, had once termed "bimbo eruptions."

It was Wright, according to Wikipedia, who "established the rapid response system that was responsible for defending Governor Clinton's record in Arkansas and promptly answering all personal attacks on the candidate."

But it was Saunders in the Chronicle who noted that Hillary Clinton's "most valuable political skill was to neutralize her husband's 'bimbo eruptions'." Saunders recalled the episode of CBS' 60 Minutes in 1992 when Hillary and Bill were interviewed and he acknowledged some infidelities during their marriage.

However, he "denied having an affair with singer Gennifer Flowers - a false denial, it turns out. In 1998, Hillary Clinton blamed the Monica Lewinsky story on a 'vast right-wing conspiracy'."

It is no "vast right-wing conspiracy" that rose up to oppose Hillary Clinton's campaign to become president, but more than 80 million gun owners who have looked at her record of support for every gun control measure to be introduced during her time in the U.S. Senate, and even before that. She campaigned on her record, and so far as gun rights activists are concerned, it is a very poor record; so poor that there had been predictions of massive turnout against her if she were to become the Democrat nominee, and as a result, that opposition could "trickle down" to Democrats at the Congressional and state levels.

The same thing, of course, would apply to Barack Obama, whose voting record on guns, coupled with statements he has made in opposition to concealed carry and in support of tighter scrutiny on who may or may not own a firearm, will never be considered strong points among rural American voters. Unfortunately for many Democratic politicians, they have expressed similar views, those opinions have been quoted and their votes are on record.

Many of those Democrats labored long and hard over the past decade to re-take Congress and earn seats in state legislatures, primarily by convincing gun owners that, if elected, they would not become the gun-grabbing Democrats that the firearms community had kept out of Congressional power for 12 years.

On the subject of gun rights, Barack Obama is simply no friend of gun owners, despite efforts to soft-peddle his position, dance around it or avoid the issue altogether. The one-term state lawmaker who then was elected to the U.S. Senate merely because people opposed the carpetbagging of black conservative Alan Keyes resides in Chicago and he has made pronouncements on several occasions that he believes there should be greater restrictions on gun ownership.

Gun rights is not an issue that either Hillary or Obama wanted to discuss in too much detail on the campaign trail, and for good reason. Neither candidate really knows anything about firearms, and their views on the subject of gun ownership are all political, not based on personal experience. When they did discuss gun rights, in debates or in speeches, there was not much substance, but ample platitudes.

Their well-established positions on gun control, as opposed to their campaign rhetoric, have remained considerably out of step with the results of a Zogby International poll conducted for Associated Television news August 8-11, 2007. The results of that poll, taken with 1,020 Americans with a margin of error of +/- 3.1 percent revealed that two-thirds of the respondents do not believe any new gun control laws are needed, and only 31 percent supported the idea of passing new and tougher gun laws.

This polling data appears to have been lost on both Hillary Clinton and Barack Obama, both of whom mentioned on the campaign trail about the necessity for added restrictions, and both of whom have voted for tougher gun laws on Capitol Hill, including reinstatement of the ban on semiautomatic sport-utility rifles, which are not "assault weapons" by any expert definition.

Hillary's gun hatred

Trust conservative spitfire Ann Coulter to sum up Hillary Clinton's dislike for firearms – and as a result, one would conclude, the people who own those firearms – with a reference to author Richard Lawrence Poe's *The Seven Myths of Gun Control.*

In a December 5, 2001 column headlined "Women We'd Like to see in Burkas," Coulter observed that Hillary Diane Rodham Clinton, the feminist's feminist, perhaps the most powerful woman in American politics, just might have this "thing" about guns because, alluding to Poe, "feminists hate guns because guns remind them of men."

Whoa, there, Ann, that's a pretty deep thought, but it is a theory that just might have a little bit of traction. Among at least some feminists, there is a common attitude that guns are bad. Bring up the subject of firearms, and you are likely to elicit this reaction: "I just hate guns!" Ask why, and there may not be a cogent, reasoned answer, and certainly not one that is calm in its explanation.

In a piece that appeared December 3, 2007 on FreeRepublic.com, author Poe went into this in some detail.

"Hillary Clinton," Poe wrote, "is America's leading gun-hater. This is no secret. Her 'F' rating from the National Rifle Association merely confirms the obvious. More perplexing is why she hates guns. The explanation may lie in the teachings of Hillary's one-time political mentor Saul Alinsky."

And just who is this fellow, Alinsky?

Poe recalls that Alinsky was "a radical organizer who got his start building militant community groups in Chicago slums during the 1930s." Are those the same Chicago slums where Hillary, beating up on rival Barack Obama during a presidential primary debate in January 2008, asserted that Obama spent some time representing the interests of a fellow named Antoin "Tony" Rezko, whom Hillary said had operated a "slum landlord business?" The same Tony Rezko shown wearing a Cheshire cat grin in a rather embarrassing photograph that surfaced on Internet muckraker Matt Drudge's website just days after that debate, flanked by Hillary and Bill Clinton?

Challenged about that photograph, Hillary suffered one of those bouts of selective memory loss that seemed to plague her during the Whitewater investigation when she was First Lady.

"I don't know the man," she told NBC after the photo appeared, explaining that during her career she had appeared in thousands of pictures. "I wouldn't know him if he walked in the door."

What's that? The smartest woman in the world, the woman with experience, the woman who brought up this guy's name to verbally bitch-slap Obama in a live television debate...wouldn't know Tony Rezko if he walked in the door? Ooooookay.

(Mr. Rezko went on trial in Chicago on federal corruption charges the same week in March that Hillary Clinton came roaring back to life for the first time in her presidential campaign, figuratively kicking Barack Obama's backside in three of four state primaries – Texas, Ohio and Rhode Island – on Tuesday March 4, 2008. Her "second resurrection, of course, was her big victory in the Pennsylvania primary on April 22. The trial became something of a sideshow issue in the campaign because of Obama's links to him.)

While Hillary may be able to feign not knowing Tony Rezko, other than to smear him as a slum lord, she certainly could not claim a memory lapse when talking about Saul Alinsky. This is the man about whom she wrote her senior thesis at Wellesley College, according to Poe's column. Alinsky died in 1972, but in Poe's opinion, he certainly left an impression on then-impressionable Hillary Diane Rodham.

In 1971 Alinsky authored a book titled Rules for Radicals that still is available today on Amazon.com and remains one of its top sellers in certain book categories. It is from Alinsky's book that Poe draws his conclusions about Hillary.

Alinsky wrote that "The power of a gun may be used to enforce slavery, or to achieve freedom."

And Poe noted that Alinsky's main beef with guns was that conservatives had more of them than Leftists. That was true in 1971, and perhaps even truer today, considering the number of firearms that are now said to be in private hands, by some estimates as many as 250 million guns of all kinds.

These are the guns, in the hands and homes of Hillary's "vast Right Wing conspiracy" conservatives – you know, people who resist the idea of the "Nanny State" that Hillary Clinton and her Left liberal soulmates labor day in and day out to create and enforce in America – that Hillary dislikes. The guns that Hillary wants registered and their owners licensed. And many of these guns are the kinds of guns Hillary wants banned; the kinds of guns that – if one subscribes to the notion that the Second Amendment was written by the

Founders as the "great insurance policy against government tyranny" – stand between Hillary and her dreams of a Leftist-controlled society; guns that would come out of the closet first to resist that kind of Totalitarian drift.

"As long as the right has more guns," Poe wrote, "the left should oppose guns, Alinsky concluded."

And maybe that's exactly the view of Hillary Clinton and her Leftist colleagues who include perennial gun haters such as House Speaker Nancy Pelosi, Senators Dianne Feinstein and Barbara Boxer (all of California) and Senators Patty Murray and Maria Cantwell (both from Washington), all far Left Democrats, all feminist icons.

Recall that when Hillary ran for the Senate in 2000, she promised that she would join with Feinstein to push legislation that would have required citizens to obtain a license and pass a safety course before they would be allowed to buy a gun, a move that might have been easily challenged under the Second Amendment as putting conditions on the exercise of a fundamental civil right.

"Her policy on guns is clear," Poe wrote about Hillary Clinton, "whatever her motives may be. She seeks to disarm the American people, while arming herself to the hilt."

No Eleanor Roosevelt

Hillary Clinton has been described as the most powerful and high profile First Lady since Eleanor Roosevelt.

To paraphrase former Senator Lloyd Bentsen, who was Michael Dukakis' running mate in 1988 against George Herbert Walker Bush and Senator Dan Quayle, "The nation knew Eleanor Roosevelt. Eleanor Roosevelt was a friend to this country. Hillary is no Eleanor Roosevelt."

Far too many in this country do not know Hillary Rodham Clinton, despite overwhelming information ranging from the anecdotal to hard, cold fact. Far too many feminists and far Left liberals either don't care about, or concur with, the political and philosophical outlook of the junior senator from New York.

Hillary Clinton would speak up for civil rights, for example, provided there was a television camera and microphone handy for her to leap in front of, and provided further that she didn't get trampled by fellow New York Senator Charles Schumer, a perennial gun hater and irrepressible publicity hound.

Eleanor Roosevelt drove through the South campaigning for civil rights, without an entourage, and with something at her side that might make Hillary Clinton wince: a handgun. Mrs. Roosevelt admitted in her own memoirs, and others have since written about this, that she often carried a handgun, even while living in the White House. Eleanor Roosevelt grew up in a different time in America, a time when self-reliance was really all anyone had to rely upon outside one's family.

There is ample historic evidence that Mrs. Roosevelt knew how to use that gun, too. She learned to shoot as a young woman. As First Lady, she refused Secret Service protection. Instead, she packed that handgun in her purse.

The Second Amendment Foundation, a firearms civil rights education and legal services group based in Bellevue, Washington, has an award named for Mrs. Roosevelt. This award goes to women who use firearms in self-defense or, as in the case of Jeanne Assam, the hero of the New Life Church incident in Colorado Springs, Colorado in December 2007, in defense of someone else.

According to the Eleanor Roosevelt Center at Val-Kill's website, she was often referred to as "Mrs. Roosevelt" or "Mrs. R" but seldom as Eleanor.

On the other hand, Hillary Diane Rodham Clinton has built her public persona as "Hillary" far more than as "Mrs. Clinton."

Franklin Delano Roosevelt brought the nation out of the Great Depression and through World War II. William Jefferson Clinton brought the nation…."Monica-gate."

Eleanor Roosevelt, according to the Val-Kill website, "persuaded Congress to have a National Teacher Day."

Hillary Clinton persuaded Congress to do what? Hillary's health care program was soundly rejected. She has not written or sponsored any significant legislation while representing the citizens of New York State. As First Lady, she failed in her campaign to successfully push gun control after the Columbine High School massacre.

She did help the campaign against Proposition B in Missouri in 1999 by recording a message that went out via telephone dialer to 75,000 households that concealed carry in the "Show Me State" was "Just too dangerous for Missouri families."

Eleanor Roosevelt never expressed the slightest desire to lead America, and as a result, through her quiet deeds and words, America followed her lead through periods of financial ruin, global warfare and racial strife.

Hillary Clinton has been hungry for power and even more hungry to run America (not the same thing as leading America), and as a result, even members of her own party were grimacing at the prospect of four or eight years of a second Clinton presidency.

It is a little late in the game for Hillary Clinton to start carrying a handgun. Besides, thanks to the extremist gun control agenda that she has championed and supported, it would not be possible for her to do so as did Eleanor Roosevelt, because – depending upon where she went – she might be committing several felonies in the process.

Eleanor Roosevelt never had to pass a background check to carry her gun. She matter-of-factly just decided it was the right thing to do, for her personal freedom of movement without having to trip over Secret Service bodyguards.

Of course, Eleanor Roosevelt could go just about anywhere she wanted in the United States because…because…more people liked her.

Five

'WE NEED TO HAVE A REGISTRY THAT REALLY WORKS...'

Democrats who truly hope to attract millions of American gun owners back to their party need only look at the people they select to lead their party to understand why tens of millions of law-abiding, upstanding shooters, gun collectors, hunters, competitors and defensively-armed private citizens balk at the "invitation."

The tragedy for the party is that many of these gun owners would readily acknowledge that when they first began voting, their votes would be cast for Democrats. Over the years, the increasingly radical party position on gun rights – toned down only in recent election cycles – turned many of these gun owners into single-issue voters, driving them toward Republican or Libertarian doctrines.

When the best that Democrats, as a national party, can offer for leadership are gun banners like Hillary Diane Rodham Clinton and Barack Hussein Obama, that party has what would be diplomatically called a monumentally wide credibility gap to overcome. After all, any Democrat with functioning brain cells must acknowledge immediately the difficulty, if not the seeming impossibility, of convincing millions of gun owning fellow citizens to join them when their national leaders want to strip those same citizens of their personal property and so egregiously erode their firearm civil rights with incrementally more invasive and restrictive ordinances and statutes that the right essentially becomes a privilege.

Obama made it almost impossible in the days before the Pennsylvania Primary when he made the now-legendary remark at a private fund-raising event in the Far Left Liberal enclave of San Francisco that rural Americans – like those in rural Pennsylvania – had become bitter over their economic situation and were clinging to guns and religion. Despite his many attempts to spin his way out of that one, a neutral observer would have to scratch

45

his head and wonder "what was Obama thinking?" Many believe it was this single comment that turned many rural Pennsylvania Democrats away from his campaign and back to Hillary, giving her a ten-point victory in that race.

With that kind of gaffe – many would argue that Obama allowed his real elitist attitude to come forth in what he thought was a safe surrounding – it may be impossible for Democrats to shed the political correctness that has been fostered by, and is now festering within, the party leadership for more than a generation. Political correctness is a huge problem for Democrats through America's heartland, and sadly, they fail to see that problem through the blinders they seem to be wearing as a political organization, much like the alcoholic or drug addict who does not see that he or she has an affliction, and therefore does nothing about it.

Before going further, one might properly mention the popular definition of "political correctness" in order to put this discussion in perspective. Political Correctness was perhaps best defined by the winning entry in the 2007 contest at Texas A&M that sought out the most appropriate definition of a contemporary term as "a doctrine, fostered by a delusional, illogical minority and rabidly promoted by an unscrupulous mainstream media, which holds forth the proposition that it is entirely possible to pick up a turd by the clean end."

That clearly explains the dilemma facing Democrats: Convincing America's firearms community that the party welcomes them and their guns, while it is abundantly clear that the party has historically supported every effort to erode if not completely erase their Second Amendment rights. This is the party from whence come opponents of concealed carry statutes that put citizens on equal footing with predatory violent criminals. This is the party from whence comes the very politicians who author and support legislation at the national, state and local level to add further restrictions on every American's fundamental civil right to keep and bear arms.

As in the case of the late former President Ronald Reagan, it has been said by many gun owners, particularly those with blue collar backgrounds that included membership in a historically-Democrat leaning trade union, that "I didn't leave the Democratic Party, the party left me." At least its leadership, which has been drifting farther to the Left over the past several years, has left those blue collar gun owners.

Which brings us around to Missouri and the Proposition B campaign of 1999. This was the ballot measure that would have opened up the "Show Me State" to concealed carry, and it gives us one of the strongest indications of just where Hillary Clinton truly stands on the issues of gun rights and personal protection.

Indeed, in Hillary's case, the Missouri campaign sticks out like a proverbial sore thumb on a record of anti-gun activity because, as First Lady, she actively engaged in the effort to convince voters to reject Proposition B, thus setting back the effort of Missouri's gun rights community by a couple of years to create a sensible concealed carry statute.

Barack Obama has merely said he does not support the idea of concealed carry by private citizens. Hillary Clinton actively campaigned against it.

Missouri gun owners recall all too vividly Hillary's contribution to the anti-Proposition B campaign. According to an April 8, 1999 *New York Times* piece on the Proposition B election failure, reporter Andrew Bluth noted that in a tape recorded message that was dialed to some 75,000 households, Hillary Clinton said this about controversial measure: "It's just too dangerous for Missouri families."

Yet now Democrats in Missouri and elsewhere expect gun owners to answer their call to join their ranks, perhaps believing that gun owners have short attention spans and even shorter memories. It appears the party no longer understands, if it ever did, that you simply cannot expect to attract huge interest groups by politically stabbing them in the back repeatedly.

More importantly, maybe Democrats do not clearly understand what "Show Me" really means, not just to Missourians, but to a nation divided by a widening philosophical chasm with gun rights activists on one side and gun control extremists on the other. In order for gun owners to support a political party, they need much more than lip service from the party and its presidential aspirants, and they haven't gotten it.

The Democratic Party's inability to understand even this simple problem clarifies why Democrats cannot grasp the moral of another Missouri-born philosophy.

When it comes to convincing gun owners across the nation that Democrats will do right by them, with Hillary Clinton charting their course, they need to remember the adage coined sometime in the last century that applies so appropriately to today's political environment: "Don't piss down my back, and then tell me it's raining."

Clinging to the dogma

In the January 17, 2008 edition of the *Las Vegas Review-Journal*, the newspaper's "In the Outdoors" columnist Doug Nielsen alluded to a remark by Hillary Clinton in the Democratic debate from the night before in which she tried to have her political cake and eat it, too.

"Well, I am against illegal guns," she stated, "and illegal guns are the cause of so much death and injury in our country. I also am a political realist, and I understand that the political winds are very powerful against doing enough to try to get guns off the street, get them out of the hands of young people. ... You know, I believe in the Second Amendment. People have a right to bear arms. But I also believe that we can common-sensically (sic) approach this."

And her "common-sense" approach? You get that from the *Wall Street Journal's* "Notable and Quotable" column of the same date, January 17, 2008, in which Clinton – responding to debate moderator the late Tim Russert, of MSNBC– suggested that how government regulates firearms owners in New York ought to be how guns and their owners are regulated everywhere.

"The law in New York was as you state," Clinton stated, "and the law in New York has worked to a great extent. I don't want the federal government pre-empting states and cities like New York that have very specific problems.

"So here's what I would do," she continued. "We need to have a registry that really works with good information about people who are felons, people who have been committed to mental institutions like the man in Virginia Tech who caused so much death and havoc. We need to make sure that that information is in a timely manner, both collected and presented."

Hillary Diane Rodham Clinton, as president, would have pushed the notion of a national gun registry as she has done – and would likely continue to do – in the United States Senate.

Democrats are you listening? There is nothing, absolutely *nothing*, that more quickly inflames and enrages America's firearms civil rights community, especially those in the West outside of California, than suggesting that firearms ought to be registered. This is the proverbial gallon of kerosene on a fire, the match to a dynamite fuse; start promoting a national gun registry and you risk bringing every angry gun owner literally out of the woodwork and to the polling places on Election Day to throw your candidates out of office and your party out of power. Think back to November 1994 and one understands the gravity of taking this sort of position, or allowing one's candidate to profess such a philosophy.

Only Democrats who are in election-proof districts or states, such as California's Senator-for-life Dianne Feinstein and Seattle Congressman Jim McDermott's ultra-liberal 7th District can typically expect to get away with that kind of nonsense.

Yet in what may be as revealing about the Democratic Party's core principles as it is about Hillary Diane Rodham Clinton's personal beliefs, the party has not corrected her or tried to get her to moderate her positions, at least in public. That could mean the party either is afraid of Hillary and what has come to be known as the "Clinton Machine" (consisting of both Hillary and Bill), or far more likely and plausible that the party privately has never abandoned its gun control position, nor has it any intention of doing so.

After all, where has the party been on the statements of Barack Obama? There was certainly no rush to condemn his remarks about "god and guns" voters in Pennsylvania. Nobody in the party has stepped forward to challenge Obama's statements on gun rights versus his votes and past positions on gun control.

America's firearms owners are regularly portrayed as caricatures; ignorant rednecks with beer bellies who abuse their wives and children, lack formal education and have no political savvy. For many on the ultra Far Left, the caricature has become reality, in that they actually believe gun owners are foolish enough to succumb to empty promises if the sales pitch is delivered properly.

That is why it has become universally acceptable for Democrat front runners to do as Hillary Clinton and Barack Obama have done, insisting that they "support" and "believe in" the Second Amendment. That could mean a lot of different things to different people, and there is always a "but..." at the end of any Second Amendment endorsement.

"I support the Second Amendment, but..." plays like a broken record.

Many politicians, including Hillary Clinton and Barack Obama, would have one believe that the Second Amendment is about rifles for hunting deer and shotguns for hunting ducks.

Indeed, at least one organization founded specifically for the purpose of fragmenting the firearms community and delivering gullible gun owners to the Democrat Party, seems to foster this approach. The Union Sportsmen's Alliance (USA), a group founded by the Theodore Roosevelt Conservation Partnership, works to turn hunters toward environmental conservationism and turn them away from conservative gun rights activism. Environmental conservationism is a subliminal philosophy that promotes the idea of accepting as a matter-of-fact the incremental loss of hunting and fishing opportunity, to the ultimate point of having essentially no hunting or fishing, or such limited opportunities as to make them out of reach for most people. Typical American sportsmen and women, however, believe that fish and wildlife agencies should work to enhance fish and game resources and expand fishing and hunting opportunities, so that anglers can put more fish in the creel and more game in the cooler. At least one of the member organizations – the Sheet Metal Workers' International Association – was quick to endorse Hillary Diane Rodham Clinton in her run for the presidency, despite the fact that she has worked to strip American gun owners, including those who belong to this union, of their gun rights. They called Clinton "the SMART choice." Gun rights activists can justifiably ask how stupid is that?

The Union Sportsmen's Alliance puts the interests of labor unions far ahead of the rights of their gun owning members, critics argue. Leaders in this group may "talk a good game," and may insist that USA is non-political, but when the group was created early in 2007, it was largely due to the unions' realization that the National Rifle Association and other gun rights organizations were communicating with union members, and explaining that many pro-union politicians habitually voted against the firearm rights of those same union members.

The Union Sportsmen's Alliance should not be confused with the American Hunters and Shooters Association, the brainchild of a Democrat support group, which will be discussed elsewhere.)

Handguns rarely enter into the discussion among these so-called "pro-gun" Democrat party leaders, except as an object for regulation, registration and derision. Forget entirely about semiautomatic rifles with black synthetic stocks because Hillary, Obama and others on the Far Left do not believe American citizens should own such firearms, and their records demonstrate that.

Yet many gun rights scholars would argue that it is the so-called "black guns" and handguns that are specifically protected from infringement by the Second Amendment, because these are the guns most likely to be pressed into service by the militia. Mention this to a gun control proponent, however, and one typically elicits a response of condescension amounting in so many words to: "You ignorant boob. We have an Army and National Guard for that."

Such gun control proponents, and particularly politicians and political candidates, would also quickly insist that they "support" the Second Amendment right to own a hunting rifle or shotgun.

And the position of NRA, the Second Amendment Foundation, Citizens Committee for the Right to Keep and Bear Arms, Gun Owners of America, Jews for the Preservation of Firearms Ownership?

"The Second Amendment is NOT about hunting."

Gun Control as Health Care

Gun control fanatics have long labored to package their crusade against firearms in many different ways in order to soft-sell the effort to millions of Americans, many of whom unwittingly succumb to the rhetoric.

How many times have you heard "It's for the children?" Hillary Clinton's early efforts in support of gun control have frequently framed this debate in terms of child safety.

In 1993, when Hillary was deeply involved in pushing her socialized health care agenda in Congress – she was described by writer Jim Schneider as "the point man on health care" in her husband's administration, in a piece he authored in Shooting Industry Magazine's December 1993 issue headlined "The year gun control became a health-care issue" – it became clear that she was not simply concerned about measles, mumps, colds and flu.

Schneider recalled how, on September 28, 1993, Hillary Clinton "told Rep. Mel Reynolds (D, Ill.), who is sponsoring his own tax-the-guns bill, that she does indeed favor a tax on firearms but that first she would like to see various categories of firearms banned."

"Two days later," Schneider reported, "she reaffirmed her desire to tax firearms under questioning in the Senate."

Congressman Mel Reynolds was a genuine piece of work. A perennial anti-gunner from the Second Congressional District of Illinois who served from 1993 to 1995, Reynolds wound up in prison, first for having sex with a 16-year-old campaign volunteer, according to a short biography, and subsequently for bank fraud. In April 1997, Reynolds was convicted on 15 counts of bank fraud – his wife, Marisol, was also charged – and sentenced to 78 months in a federal prison. This was after his August 1995 conviction for solicitation of child pornography, sexual assault and obstruction of justice. He was in jail when the federal bank fraud indictment was handed down, according to Wikipedia.

Reynolds' sentence was commuted, however, by President Bill Clinton – perhaps a sympathy gesture toward another Democrat who got caught having sex with a subordinate – after having served 42 months.

While Reynolds will not be serving more time in prison, or another term in Congress to push even more anti-gun schemes, fortunes have been better for Hillary Clinton, who never gave up on the notion of guns as a health care problem.

Hillary has lots of friends. Schneider noted in his column that USA Today editorialized in its October 1, 1993 edition that "Gun control and health reform go hand in hand. Indeed, gun violence is a steady and powerful inflater of health costs."

"In 1985, the total medical costs of gun violence were more than $900 million," Schneider further quoted the newspaper. "Three years later, the costs had risen to $1.2 billion. Low-ball figures for 1990 place the number at $1.4 billion. And costs surely are continuing to rise ...

"This is why President Clinton plugged gun control in his health-care speech.

"It's why Hillary Rodham Clinton, after opposing the idea, indicated ... that she supports a plan to more than double the 10 percent gun manufacturers' excise tax to help pay for health reform ..."

But Schneider had done his homework on the issue, and he concluded his remarks by noting that, "the fact is that gun violence is responsible for a fraction of 1 percent of the total amount spent on medical care in this country (an estimated $752 billion in 1991). Of course, following this logic, shouldn't there be a hefty health tax on automobiles? Far more medical costs arise from car accidents than the misuse of firearms."

Of course, the issue really was never about covering the costs of health care, it was about ratcheting down on gun owners any way possible, including adding a substantial tax to the price of firearms to pay for the health care of shooting victims in crimes they did not commit.

And in that regard, Hillary Diane Rodham Clinton has always been out front when there was an anti-gun law to promote or a pro-gun law to oppose, which brings us back to Missouri and the campaign to pass a concealed carry measure in 1999.

This was a political bare knuckles battle championed by the NRA, which had hired consultant Fred Myers to coordinate the Proposition B campaign. Myers had been involved in the successful 1997 effort in Washington State to defeat Initiative 676, perhaps the most anti-gun measure ever placed on a ballot. It was crushed in a vote that produced a lopsided 71 percent public vote supporting the Evergreen State's gun rights.

But in Missouri, Myers could not counter the Hillary Rodham Clinton influence with that taped message about safety in Missouri homes being dependent upon defeat of Proposition B.

Myers would later surface as a leader of the previously-mentioned Union Sportsmen's Alliance, a rather curious turn of events because he is no fan of anti-gun politicians.

But it was during Hillary Clinton's term as First Lady that the gun control movement began fine-tuning its rhetoric. When guns were not a health care problem, restrictive gun control legislation became "common sense" or "sensible" legislation. And it was always "modest."

After Proposition B was defeated in Missouri, Sarah Brady, chairwoman of then-Handgun Control, Inc. (later to become the Brady Campaign to Prevent Gun Violence), was quoted in newspapers stating, "The idea of putting more guns on the street is just a disaster, and this vote shows people agree with that. People in Missouri understood that this would've allowed people to take guns into bars and stadiums and made the streets much more dangerous. Common sense prevailed."

Remember earlier in this chapter where Hillary Clinton, under questioning in the December 16, 2007 debate, said people must "common-sensically" (sic) approach the issue of gun control versus gun rights. Remarks like this certainly make her no friends in the gun rights movement – whether she believes otherwise or not – but ultimately, as a member of what some see as the Democrat party's ultra-Left ruling wing, it may not concern Hillary that gun owners dislike her. Pandering remarks about "support" for the Second Amendment notwithstanding, one suspects from her record that Hillary Clinton genuinely dislikes gun owners.

But does Hillary Clinton stand alone as a Democrat on this? No.

Rival Barack Hussein Obama, the Chicago Democrat who has also apparently never met an anti-gun measure he didn't like, also had some comments on the subject during that January 16 debate. Responding to remarks about the registration of gun owners, he acknowledged, "I don't think we can get that done."

But then he added, "here's the broader context that I think is important for us to remember: We essentially have two realities, when it comes to guns in this country. You've got the tradition of lawful gun ownership; that all of us, as we travel around rural parts of the country. And it is very important for many Americans to be able to hunt, fish, take their kids out, teach them how to shoot. And then you've got the reality of 34 Chicago public school students who get shot down on the streets of Chicago.

"We can reconcile those two realities by making sure the Second Amendment is respected and that people are able to lawfully own guns," Obama continued, "but we also start cracking down on the kinds of abuses of firearms that we see on the streets."

Only John Edwards, a Democrat who once told an interviewer that he believes owning a handgun should be a privilege, seemed to understand how American firearms owners look at this dilemma. Regarding licensing and registration, Edwards bluntly told Russert, "I'm against it. Having grown up where I did in the rural South, everyone around me had guns, everyone hunted. And I think it is enormously important to protect people's Second Amendment rights.

But then Edwards kept talking, which is never a good idea for a politician, and he reinserted his foot in mouth to the nation's gun owners when he added, "I don't believe that means you need an AK-47 to hunt. And I think the assault weapons ban, which Hillary spoke about...as president of the United States, I'll do everything in my power to reinstate it. But I do think we need a president who understands the sportsmen; hunters who use their guns for lawful purposes have a right to have their Second Amendment rights looked after."

Well, how magnanimous! All three Democrats offer lip service to a fundamental civil right and then confess that they will look at more restrictions, and they get a pass.

Contrast these remarks with those from Sen. John McCain, a Republican also in the race for president (and destined to become the party's nominee) and someone who has not garnered much trust from gun owners over the past few years. McCain, co-author with Sen. Joseph Lieberman of a piece of legislation aimed at gun shows, still seemed to get it right when he remarked on his website, "Gun control is a proven failure in fighting crime. Law-abiding citizens should not be asked to give up their rights because of criminals – criminals who ignore gun laws anyway."

McCain's track record, just for the sake of comparison, has actually been the polar opposite of Hillary Clinton and Barack Obama. He voted against the ban on so-called "assault weapons" and he has opposed waiting periods for gun purchases. Yet, in his legislation with the ultra-liberal (on every issue but the Iraq war) Lieberman, McCain would have mandated background checks on all firearms transactions at gun shows, not just those conducted by licensed firearms dealers.

And what about licensed gun dealers? Responding to Russert during the January 16, 2008 debate, Hillary Clinton stated, "We do need to crack down on illegal gun dealers. This is something that I would like to see more of. And we need to enforce the laws that we have on the books. I would also work to reinstate the assault-weapons ban. We now have, once again, police deaths going up around the country, and in large measure because bad guys now have assault weapons again. We stopped it for awhile. Now they're back on the streets."

However, Clinton acknowledged that as a presidential candidate, she had "backed off" a plan to license gun owners and register guns.

Meanwhile, Obama contends that getting access to sensitive gun trace data maintained by the Bureau of Alcohol, Tobacco, Firearms and Explosives will somehow contribute to a reduction in criminal activity. He suggested as much during the January 16 debate.

Guns Break Elections

For a political animal with the savvy of a Hillary Diane Rodham Clinton, one might be apprehensive about continuing to even vaguely support the notion of gun control or gun registration, but then again, that's presuming one does not have it set in her mind that being selected as her party's candidate for president of the United States is more of a coronation than a nomination.

It was sagely noted in the October 23, 2007 edition of the *Des Moines, Iowa Register* that "Republican and Democratic presidential candidates dance upon political eggshells when it comes to gun control because it's a divisive issue that can change the outcome of an election."

The newspaper noted that popular opinion suggests Al Gore lost the 2000 election on the gun issue, and there is much statistical data to back that up. Gore did not carry his home state of Tennessee, and he lost West Virginia and other states on the gun issue.

Of course, the National Rifle Association takes great pains, along with other gun rights organizations, to promote the belief among political candidates that being on the wrong side of the gun issue means a quick retirement from public office. Even NRA's quietly glib spokesman Andrew Arulanandam was quoted by the Des Moines newspaper observing, "What you have is some of the Democratic candidates who know this issue will be a liability. Their support of gun control in the past could prove to be a loser for them in the general election, and that is why they would rather not make it an issue."

Too bad, because it is an issue, and will always be an issue to one degree or another, simply because about half the households in the United States have at least one firearm, and there are tens of millions of gun owners who will resist attempts to take their guns. As the election of 1994 made abundantly clear, when gun owners get very angry – which is what they became after the Clinton Administration pushed through the Brady Law and the ban on so-called "assault weapons" and standard capacity ammunition magazines – Democrats wake up on the morning after election day wondering what train hit them.

This explains why even Democrat leaders including Charles Schumer, the senior senator from New York who once crowed that his party would become the NRA's worst nightmare following passage of the Brady Law, have muzzled themselves. Even Schumer has stated that he "supports the Second Amendment" but his track record belies that claim in the eyes of millions of Americans.

One revelation out of the Bill Clinton administration was how much influence polls had on the disgraced former president. Perhaps Hillary Diane Rodham Clinton has also been paying attention to polls, particularly one done for Associated Television News by Zogby International that was released on August 21, 2007.

According to that poll, which contacted 1,020 Americans between August 8 and 11, and had a margin of error of plus/minus 3.1%, two-thirds of American voters rejected the idea that new gun control laws are required. Only 31 % of those polled said they supported new, tougher gun laws, Zogby reported at the time. Sixty-six percent said they believed enforcement of existing laws would be sufficient, and that sentiment ran across all demographic groups and in all regions of the country, with the exceptions being, according to Zogby, Asian and liberal voters.

For Hillary Clinton, running in 2000 for the open Senate seat in New York against Republican Rep. Rick Lazio, that would not have been important because all she needed was to get the popular vote in New York City and on Long Island to win election, and there is strong anti-gun sentiment among those constituencies. In upstate New York and out west toward Lakes Ontario and Erie, that is not the case, but voters there are outnumbered and all-too-often ignored.

When running for a narrow constituency in downstate New York, it is safe to tell crowds in Manhattan that you support the licensing of handguns and their owners. Try that in Missoula, Montana, Phoenix, Arizona or Salt Lake City, Utah and it is a different situation entirely. And that probably explains why Hillary Clinton publicly "backed away" from the issue of licensing and registration, because she was no longer simply trying to convince a collective of New Yorkers to put her in office. She was trying to sell herself as palatable to Americans across the country, and that requires verbal restraint and re-packaging.

Still, for her to suggest during a presidential primary debate that "we need to have a registry that really works" indicates that Hillary Clinton remained convinced at the time that not only did she have a party nomination essentially sewed up –the subsequent results of a Super Tuesday 2008 election suggested a race between her and Barack Obama was still close – she was also convinced that she could get away with remarks like that because America was going to put her in office just to have a change from George W. Bush.

But at the 2008 Shooting, Hunting and Outdoor Trade Show – the firearms industry's largest such gathering, held in Las Vegas, Nevada – there was strong evidence that every effort would be made to hold Hillary Clinton accountable for her remarks. That effort would include reminding American gun owners that during the first half of the Bill Clinton administration's first term, when voters got "two for the price of one," that gun control was, as Wikipedia put it, "a major political issue."

There is nothing to suggest that Hillary Clinton was not very involved in that earlier effort, and even less to suggest that the first half of a Hillary Clinton presidency would not mirror the activities of her husband's first two year years. Perhaps only the memory of what happened to Bill Clinton's Congressional supporters in 1994 might temper Hillary Clinton, Barack Obama and other Democrats who claim to have moderated their positions on gun control, but have, in fact, only toned down their rhetoric.

Six

'JUST SAY 'NO' TO GUN RIGHTS'

Andrew P. Napolitano, senior judicial analyst for Fox News and author of *The Constitution in Exile* and *Constitutional Chaos*, was in a discussion with Fox commentator Bill O'Reilly on the latter's syndicated radio talk show on Friday, January 11, 2006.

O'Reilly's "The Radio Factor" is pretty much like his television program, in which he typically dominates any conversation with a guest, but on this day Judge Napolitano would mention something that – to gun rights activists – was chilling. Never one to beat around the bush, Napolitano waded right into his host's comments on electronic eavesdropping by the government, under provisions of the controversial Patriot Act.

According to a partial transcript of that exchange, posted online by Media Matters.org two days later, O'Reilly did not indicate concern about the eavesdropping, even after Napolitano interjected, "Would you feel this way if Hillary were president?"

O'Reilly's response: "Yeah."

But then Napolitano shot right back, asserting, "Because then, you know, the pro-life and the pro-gun (groups) will – they'll be targets of warrantless searches."

O'Reilly interjected briefly, "No, but...not unless they're dealing..."

He was interrupted by Napolitano, who added, "And maybe conservative commentators will be targets of warrantless searches."

Napolitano is not a person to launch frivolous tirades on live radio, and in early 2006, when it was a fairly common presumption that Hillary Diane Rodham Clinton would soon toss her bonnet into the presidential campaign, he and others started looking at the potential of a second Clinton presidency. Considering her performance as First Lady during her husband's tarnished term in office, the firearms community has looked at Hillary from a jaded angle, and overwhelmingly, gun rights activists dislike what they see.

While it is clear to many observers that Hillary Clinton's views about

57

gun ownership are far out in left field, she moderated those positions for the benefit of her presidential campaign, at least, and in the process, found herself surpassed in the realm of gun control advocacy. Democrat Sen. Barack Obama has left no doubt that he is even farther to the Left on gun rights, consistently casting votes on anti-gun legislation that mirrored Clinton's positions in the Senate, with but one exception. When Hillary Clinton became one of 16 senators who voted against legislation that prohibits gun grabs like the ones following Hurricane Katrina in New Orleans, Obama voted for that bill. Like Hillary, Obama has also insisted that "there is an individual right to bear arms, but it's subject to common sense regulation."

"Common sense regulation" typically involves background checks and other restrictions that tend to make the Second Amendment civil right look more like a privilege. Obama considers the handgun ban in Washington, D.C. to be a "common sense" regulation, according to his campaign staff.

Still, when it comes to being on the wrong side of gun rights, Hillary Clinton has a far longer track record than Barack Obama, and gun owners have long memories (combined with short fuses).

Take a look back at October 1993 when, as First Lady, Hillary Clinton flew to New Jersey to support anti-gun Gov. Jim Florio, a tax-and-spend Liberal who endorsed a ban on so-called "assault weapons" and backed other restrictive gun measures. Mrs. Clinton joined Florio on a campaign sweep through southern New Jersey that day, praising Florio's stand on gun control.

The *New York Times'* Robert Hanley quoted Clinton's speech about Florio in a piece published in the October 31 edition, in which she noted, "He stood up to the forces that have profited from the violence that has stalked our streets too long."

Even then, she was quick to excuse her anti-gun politicking as an effort on behalf of children.

"This is a battle for the future of our children," she claimed. "This is a battle for the safety of women."

Florio lost his bid for re-election to a woman, Christine Todd Whitman.

No matter; Hillary had made her points with the Left, and she was learning about stump speeches in front of crowds.

At the same time, prominent leaders in the gun rights camp were learning about Hillary, and how effective she could be as a speaker in front of the right audience in a friendly environment.

Years later, as Hillary warmed up her campaign to become the first woman president of the United States, National Rifle Association Executive Vice President Wayne LaPierre would write, "Both leading Democratic candidates, Obama and Hillary, are supporters of firearms bans. For Clinton, that includes the confiscations that took place in New Orleans in the wake of Hurricane Katrina. Hillary has pushed vigorously for a harsher version of

Bill Clinton's semi-auto ban, a hallmark of their 'co-Presidency' and a stark reminder of what 1600 Pennsylvania Avenue would have in store for you upon the return of this 'political team'."

LaPierre minced no words: "In seeking to capture the White House in November 2008, both Hillary Clinton and Barack Obama are lying in saying they support the Second Amendment."

The NRA chief then recalled Hillary's demand for handgun licensing and registration at the 2000 Million Mom March rally on Mother's Day. Then, quoting the *New York Times*, LaPierre spotlighted Hillary's anti-gun agenda, which included a promise to work with anti-gun California Sen. Dianne Feinstein on a measure that would require "prospective gun buyers" to get a license and take a safety course.

This was legislation that would have required the creation of a national gun registry.

Early in the presidential campaign, in an Associated Press report by Calvin Woodward dated April 18, 2007, he noted at the time that Hillary – apparently using New York gun laws as her model – "also supported proposals for state-issued photo gun licenses, as well as a national registry for handgun sales." These are the same positions she held in 2000 during her first successful run for the Senate.

Hillary may have changed her rhetoric, but it never appeared through the entire 2008 presidential primary campaign that she had changed her position.

The One-Name Celebrity

Whatever else Hillary Diane Rodham Clinton may or may not be, it becomes immediately obvious that her campaign has promoted her as some kind of celebrity, intended to be known primarily by her first name only: Hillary. Check the campaign signs. "Hillary" is prominently displayed, with little emphasis, if any, on her last name: Clinton.

Whether she seeks to subliminally distance herself from her husband, there is something about people in public life who try to establish themselves by merely a first name. Oprah! Cher! Rosie!

And now, Hillary!

In all fairness, an adoring fan base has long called the senator by her first name only, even when she was First Lady. When she departed the White House early, ostensibly to run for the senate in New York, but just as likely to separate from her husband during the Lewinsky scandal, she quickly emerged as "Hillary" on the New York campaign trail.

One might reasonably ask the senator whether she sees herself as a representative of the citizens of New York State on Capitol Hill, or whether she sees herself as a celebrity with a job in Washington, D.C. After all, we're discussing the woman who, during an appearance on the Tyra Banks Show on January 18, 2008, she revealed a desire to appear on *Dancing with the Stars*, without making it clear whether she would be the "star," or want to dance with someone else who is.

(Of course, the rise of the politician-as-celebrity might date back to the days when Richard Nixon, prior to his election as president in 1968, appeared on Rowan and Martin's Laugh-In, exclaiming "Sock It To Me," not to mention Bill Clinton's pre-presidential appearances playing a saxophone, or appearances on Saturday Night Live by Republicans John McCain and Mike Huckabee.)

Early in the 2008 presidential campaign, her supporters in the media and in Hollywood seemed convinced that the Democratic Party nomination would actually translate to Hillary Clinton's coronation as the next president. But then came Barack Obama, and as the winter primaries left him with repeated victories while her campaign floundered with message and money problems, the shine reportedly came off of Hillary's campaign tactics, as well as her personality, at least behind closed doors and certainly away from public attention.

Granted, following her resurgence in the March 4 primaries that brought her wins in Ohio, Texas and Rhode Island – making Hillary as much of a "comeback kid" as her husband had been 16 years previously – she perked right up.

As noted in previous chapters, Hillary Clinton campaigned vigorously against gun rights while she served as First Lady, not only in New Jersey but out in Missouri, where her opposition to Proposition B – the concealed carry measure – left Show Me State gun owners with long-simmering resentment toward her and the Democrat Party.

Democrats simply cannot shake their reputation for being the party of gun control, and part of the reason for that is due to the involvement of prominent Democrat politicians like Hillary Clinton in anti-gun efforts. No matter the issue, be it handgun bans, one-gun-a-month schemes, microstamping handguns, handgun ammunition and bullets or opposition to concealed carry, it has traditionally been Democrats at the head of the campaign.

In early 2008, Democrats again seized the opportunity to look rather bad to gun rights advocates when Sen. Dianne Feinstein of California and Rep. Norm Dicks of Washington state mounted an effort to stop Interior Secretary Dirk Kempthorne from changing national park rules to allow legally-licensed private citizens to carry sidearms for personal protection inside park boundaries. Loaded guns had been banned for some 70 years in the parks, ostensibly to prevent poaching, but in recent years with crime statistics on the rise in national parks and the passage of concealed carry statutes in dozens of states, attitudes about the issue changed.

Indeed, 51 senators – half of the U.S. Senate body – signed a letter to

Kempthorne in December 2007 supporting a change in rules to allow citizens to legally carry concealed handguns in the parks. Hillary Clinton was not one of them.

There was something else about the 1999 Missouri campaign when she was still First Lady that gives a strong indication about how Hillary Clinton would politicize the Department of Justice.

Critics of the Bill Clinton administration have widely held that Hillary had far too much influence, if not total control, over the selection of the attorney general. She wanted a woman in that position, and the country got one: Janet Reno. This was after Clinton's first two nominees, Zoe Baird and Kimba Wood, had to withdraw because they had both been revealed to have employed illegal immigrants.

But under Janet Reno, as recalled in the Wikipedia account of the Proposition B election campaign, both U.S. attorneys in Missouri were allowed to actively campaign against the ballot issue. They were also allowed to use Justice Department facilities and the agency name to lobby against the measure.

This was an outrage to Missouri gun owners, who argued that the federal Justice Department had no business at all trying to influence a state ballot issue, on gun rights or anything else.

But this seemed hardly out of the ordinary for federal attorneys under Janet Reno's supervision.

Two years before the 1999 Proposition B campaign in Missouri, voters in another state – Washington – also faced a gun measure on their ballot, only this one was arguably the most Draconian anti-gun proposition ever put up to a public vote (which undoubtedly is why it failed miserably). This was Initiative 676, the 1997 measure that would have required licensing and registration of all handguns in the Evergreen State, and carried stiff penalties even for police officers and their spouses, in the event of a violation.

Championing that campaign was a group calling itself Washington CeaseFire, perhaps one of the more vocal minority gun control organizations in the country, with a member base of between 3,000 and 6,000, depending upon whose estimates one accepts. (By contrast, the NRA has some 85,000 members in Washington State, and Bellevue, Washington is home to the Second Amendment Foundation and the Citizens Committee for the Right to Keep and Bear Arms, two of the more prominent national firearms civil rights organizations. The Washington Arms Collectors, a group that puts on gun shows, has some 12,000 members, yet Washington CeaseFire continually insists it represents the views of a majority of Evergreen State citizens.)

Leading Washington CeaseFire as its president at the time of the 1997 initiative campaign was Democrat Thomas Wales, an assistant federal prosecutor in the Justice Department's Seattle office. Widely considered an extremist anti-gunner, Wales was known to have done radio interviews from his office during the 1997 campaign, and during a debate on the measure at the University of Washington, Wales – in one of his more hysteria-laden moments – declared that "The NRA is against the constitution."

Rather than say "No" to gun rights in Washington State, where the state constitution contains one of the strongest individual right to bear arms provisions of any state in the country, enraged voters handed the measure a stunning defeat. When the ballots were counted, I-676 was crushed by an overwhelming 71-29 percent turnout. That the measure could not even garner a 30 percent favorable vote in a state thought to be dominated by liberal Seattle politics sent a message to the gun control lobby and Democrats in the State Legislature that the majority of Evergreen State voters, be they Republicans, Democrats, Libertarians or some other political stripe, are not enamored with extremist gun control.

Ironically and sadly, Wales was later murdered – in October 2001 – by an unknown killer as he sat at a computer in the basement of his home in Seattle's fashionable Queen Anne Hill neighborhood.

It is highly improbable that neither Barack Obama nor Hillary Clinton, as president of the United States, would pull Janet Reno out of retirement to again head the Justice Department, but what does seem clear is that either would certainly nominate someone with political views akin to their own, and that does not necessarily mean their views as expressed on the campaign trail. What that would mean in terms of how the Justice Department views the Second Amendment almost certainly would be a 180-degree shift from how the Justice Department has viewed the Amendment since former Attorney General John Ashcroft issued his memorandum under the second George Bush administration.

Ashcroft's view was that the Second Amendment protects a fundamental individual civil right. The view of the Bill Clinton administration was that the amendment only protects some "collective" right of the states to form militias.

With both Hillary and Obama joining other leading Democrats as being decidedly on the side of gun control – and "supporting" the Second Amendment while also supporting "reasonable, common-sense" restrictions on that civil right – the timing of the landmark Supreme Court decision on the District of Columbia's handgun ban and whether the amendment does affirm an individual right was paramount.

Limited Empowerment?

As sure as Barack Hussein Obama is a product of the Chicago political environment, Hillary Diane Rodham Clinton is most assuredly a product of the "women's empowerment" movement, if not one of its leaders and current architects. Incredibly, while those involved in this socio-political movement are properly concerned about domestic violence and spousal abuse, their traditionally liberal values invariably collide with the common sense of gun ownership.

According to data compiled by the Silent Witness program, "intimate homicides" declined between 1976 and 2004 by 47.6 percent overall, but 2004 actually saw the first increase in a while, up 0.7 percent, with women victims now outnumbering men by a 3-to-1 margin, where in 1976, there were 1,348 male victims and 1,596 female victims, according to Silent Witness data.

All too frequently, women find themselves on the losing end of a deadly argument or attack from an ex-boyfriend or spouse, and just as often in a tragic sense, one finds that groups battling domestic violence are supporters of strict gun control.

But consider this dilemma from a practical standpoint: If someone is being attacked by an opponent who is larger and stronger, what is the sense of admonishing the potential victim to keep away from guns, don't have one in the home, call and wait for the police (while you are being beaten, stabbed or shot)?

Do not these terrified, abused women deserve a fighting chance?

That was certainly something that Hillary Clinton avoided discussing when she delivered a speech to the First Ladies' Conference on Domestic Violence in San Salvador, El Salvador on November 17, 1998.

"For women to live free of violence," she said, "they must have access to education. It is the single most powerful tool to raise the status of women and girls and it should be the birthright of every citizen of every nation. Many women stay in abusive relationships because they are not educated and do not believe they can find their own way in the world. The more we educate women, the more we will diminish the possibility that any woman will remain the victim of domestic violence.

"For women to live free of violence," she continued, "they must have access to credit. I've seen the lives of women, from many walks of life, changed, transformed as the result of small micro credit loans. As they became more economically independent, they gained confidence to stand up for their rights in their own families and to play a greater role in their communities.

"For women to live free of violence," Hillary advised, "they must have access to health care for themselves and their children. And if they do have access to health care, they are better able to understand what they need and what they can obtain for themselves and their children and they don't feel so dependant, as they might otherwise.

"And for women to live free of violence," she stated, "we must make good on the central message of the platform for action from the UN Women's Conference in Beijing. That no nation can progress unless every citizen is valued and treated with dignity and given the opportunity to live up to his or her God-given potential."

But of all the things she thought abused women should have to avoid being abused further, Hillary Diane Rodham Clinton overlooked the equalizer, the one tool with which women can level the playing field. She did not suggest having a gun. She even avoided suggesting taking a self-defense course, having pepper spray, or utilizing some other non-lethal but forceful means of personal protection.

One might just find that a bit odd, ironic or amusing in the macabre sense, provided one believes the stories that have been floating around for several years about how Hillary Clinton is a spousal abuser who has clobbered Bill Clinton more than once, with fingernails or thrown objects.

In a May 7, 2002 column written by Glenn J. Sacks under the headline "Is There a Batterer in the US Senate?" the author refers to Hillary biographies about incidents in which the junior senator from New York has allegedly unleashed her temper. While no small number of Americans, both men and women, might easily suggest that Bill "had it coming," for all of his dalliances, such attacks still would fall under the definition of "domestic violence."

Sacks alluded to one 1993 incident in which Hillary allegedly scratched Bill's face deeply with her fingernails along his jaw line.

In another incident, ignited by the Monica Lewinsky revelations, Hillary allegedly assaulted Bill on August 13, 1999. Quoting author Christopher Andersen's *Bill and Hillary*, Sacks wrote that the former president was left "weeping (and) begged her forgiveness." It was during that fray that Hillary allegedly screamed at Bill that he was a "stupid, stupid, stupid bastard."

"Bill Clinton," Sacks wrote, "handled the incidents in a manner eerily reminiscent of the way many female victims of domestic violence did in the pre-feminist era. Ashamed, he tried to cover the incidents up, even ordering his representatives to publicly alibi his wife's violence. He probably blamed himself for 'provoking' her, as if marital infidelity warrants physical assault. And he almost certainly never considered calling the police or formally charging his abuser."

In 2004, Hillary Clinton joined with the anti-gun front group, Americans for Gun Safety, to push for tougher gun law restrictions in cases of domestic violence or protection orders. Also involved in this effort was the National Network Against Domestic Violence. They want the authorities to crack down on the gun rights of anyone slapped with a protection order.

NBC News reported at the time that "nearly a third of all women killed in the United States in 2000 were killed by their current or former lovers. Guns were used in most of those homicides."

Yet with all of this information, Hillary Clinton has failed to support a woman's right to choose...not to be a victim. When Hillary is quoted on the NARAL Pro-Choice America website supporting *Roe v. Wade*, she noted, "I believe in the freedom of women to make their own decisions about the most personal and significant matters affecting their lives."

Odd that she would not openly support a woman's right to decide whether to own a gun for self-defense, which most certain falls under the definition of "personal and significant matters affecting their lives." While she advocated that "abortion should be safe, legal and rare," she has worked steadfastly with such groups as the Americans for Gun Safety Foundation and the Brady Campaign to Prevent Gun Violence, both of which work hard to make it increasingly difficult for law-abiding private citizens, including domestic violence victims, to buy firearms and obtain concealed carry licenses.

Words versus Deeds

The true measure of Hillary Clinton's attitude about guns – any kind of guns – is evident not by listening to what she says about "supporting" the Second Amendment, but what she has done on virtually every level, including the effort she spearheaded to derail the appointment of Mary Sheila Gall as chairman of the Consumer Product Safety Commission.

Gall had served on the commission under Ann Brown, who had been appointed to the chair by President Clinton. Brown has been described as an "activist" while Gall was more reserved in her actions regarding products.

According to a profile of the dispute that appeared on the ConsumerAffairs. com website, Brown was a "consumer advocate" for some 20 years before being appointed to the commission by Bill Clinton. That included almost 15 years as vice president of the Consumer Federation of America, and serving as chairman of the board of Public Voice, a consumer advocacy group.

Gall, according to the same report, served two years as Assistant Secretary of the Department of Health and Human Services under the first Bush administration. She "headed the Human Development Services Agency" and "oversaw a yearly budget of five billion dollars and a workforce of 1,000 employees." Before she was appointed to the Assistant Secretary post, Gall was counselor to the Director of the Office of Personnel Management, working "directly with the White House Cabinet Council, other federal agencies, federal labor unions and public interest organizations..." She had also chaired the President's Task Force on Adoption under Ronald Reagan.

It was no secret that Brown and Gall, the latter appointed to the commission in 1991 by the first President Bush, did not agree on some issues, including baby bath seats, baby walkers and...BB guns.

The problem with the baby bath seats, as well as the baby walkers, appears to have been more a matter of poor parental supervision than product failure, at least from Gall's perspective. The dispute is described in a story from April 2001 (still found on the ConsumerAffairs.com website) in which it was revealed that at the time, at least 67 infant deaths had been linked to the bath seats.

These seats, which Brown wanted to ban, were designed to make bathing an infant easier, but if left unattended, infants could slide out and drown. It should be noted that drownings kill far more young children in the 1-4 year age group than firearms mishaps according to data from Child Health USA.

While Brown wanted a ban, Gall contended that the problem was with the parents. Likewise, in their disagreement over baby walkers, Gall opposed regulating the devices, again arguing that it is up to parents to more closely supervise their toddlers.

And then came the disagreement over Daisy airguns.

Two days before Brown departed as chairman, and after Gall's nomination to succeed her had been rejected on a partisan vote, the outgoing "activist" chairwoman engineered a vote aimed at the recall of Daisy Powerline BB guns.

Over the years, there have been many injuries attributed to one type of BB gun or another. This time around, the controversy surrounded an airgun model that had been previously examined by the Consumer Product Safety Commission several times, with no finding of a defect. The guns worked as they were supposed to, and this was pointed out by Gall, according to several accounts of the controversy.

Gall had, as reported at the time in an alert from the NRA's Institute for Legislative Action to NRA members, cited several reasons for opposing the recall plan. NRA noted at the time that "The greatest threat posed by this action is that the arguments used to portray the BB guns as 'defective' could be used against a variety of cartridge firearms in current or prospective litigation."

The NRA alert quoted an attorney for the gun control lobby, who had told the Reuters news agency, "We have made no secret that we think there ought to be consumer oversight of guns...BB guns could be a step in the right direction."

Naturally, Hillary would justify her opposition to Gall's appointment as being in the interests of children. This strategy was perhaps best described in an article found on the website of The American Cause on August 2, 2001. In that piece, the group noted with no attempt to hide their disgust and sarcasm, "Meet Mary Sheila Gall, President Bush's choice to head the Consumer Product Safety Commission and latest target of Senator Hillary. The Queen of Chappaqua isn't a member of the Commerce Committee, yet she's leading the charge to discredit Gall. Her battle cry: the one-size-fits-all Clinton reason – 'for the children.' For the state would be more accurate."

Gall's problem with many liberals was that she historically had resisted regulating products where she felt it wasn't necessary. She had essentially accused Brown of trying to create a "federal Nanny State" on her watch at the commission, which was not unlike criticisms leveled at Hillary Clinton when the-then First Lady claimed that raising children "takes a village." (Clinton critics at the time were quick to fire back that "it takes a village idiot" anytime Hillary came up with some new initiative, and especially when she defended her highly unpopular health care plan.)

The fact that Gall had opposed launching a process by which the Daisy airguns could be recalled was, perhaps, the last straw for liberals on Capitol Hill. Gall's nomination was derailed four months after it was offered by President Bush, and Hillary Clinton led that charge.

Whether Hillary Clinton disguises her anti-gun efforts as being in the interest of child safety, crime reduction or defense of abused women, the common denominator is the firearm, or anything that looks like it or encourages someone to become interested in guns. And that would include air rifles.

Despite her insistence that she is a "Second Amendment supporter," she has never taken a vote or said anything of significance that even remotely suggests she understands what the Second Amendment is really all about. It is not about hunting ducks.

Seven

FACING, AND FAILING, THE 'ACID TEST'

Throughout the past quarter-century at least, and maybe longer, Democrats at all levels of government, even down to county commissions and most assuredly state legislatures, have been far more likely to embrace gun control positions than Republicans, Independents and Libertarians.

One might flippantly declare that "they drink the same Kool Aid" but this attitude about guns and the people who own them seems to be a cornerstone of the Democrat philosophy and it runs to the extreme. How extreme? Consider the observation of California Congressman Henry Waxman, a fellow with something of a pug nose underlined by a thick but closely-cropped moustache. Because of this, when he looks at people, it always appears as though he is looking down his nose at them.

Waxman – like so many of his fellow Democrats – simply does not trust citizens with firearms, especially if those citizens are capable of explaining why the Second Amendment was included by the Founders in the Bill of Rights; that it is an "insurance policy" against dictatorial government.

The chairman of the House Oversight and Government Reform Committee, Waxman once was quoted observing, "If someone is so fearful that, that they're going to start using their weapons to protect their rights, makes me very nervous that these people have these weapons at all."

On another occasion, the NRA "F-rated" Liberal from California's 30th District – a career politician who has served in Congress more than 30 years – told a press conference, "Our current gun laws are so weak that our country serves as a virtual arsenal for terrorists."

Now, that's an odd statement from a man who, according to the non-partisan "OnTheIssues.com" website, voted against legislation in 2005 that would have allowed the president to clamp down on foreign arms shipments to China by allowing the president to take sanctions against anyone who violated the embargo. But nobody ever accused Liberal Democrats of being consistent.

That Bill and Hillary Clinton would be strong supporters of gun control should be no surprise at all.

Likewise, Barack Obama, having cut his political teeth in the Chicago area under the tutelage of the anti-gun Richard Daley political machine, and at one time reportedly considered a job as president of the anti-gun Joyce Foundation, would be a surprise indeed if he were not a gun control disciple.

Gun control still remains something of a central theme with the Democratic Party, and if one doubts that, take a look at what happened to the presidential aspirations of New Mexico Gov. Bill Richardson, the most pro-gun Democrat in the 2008 field. He finished way behind and called it quits after disappointing showings in state Democratic primaries, an indication of how much support among the party faithful there is for someone who ushered a concealed carry statute through his state's legislature not long after taking office.

It was surprising because Richardson's Hispanic roots would otherwise make him a genuine front-runner among Democrats seeking to appeal to one of the largest and growing voting blocs in the country.

But the 2008 presidential campaign was full of surprises, with Richardson igniting a political blood feud with Bill Clinton over the New Mexico governor's endorsement of Barack Obama, the man who does not approve of concealed carry because he is afraid too many citizens might ultimately get hurt. Richardson had served in two positions in the Clinton Administration, and Bill and Hillary had lobbied him hard – too hard as it turned out – to endorse the former First Lady. That evidently was what drove him to endorse Obama, along with the sense he got from listening to both Clintons that they somehow felt entitled to not only get the nomination, but to win back the White House.

Aristocracies and political dynasties do not enjoy a warm reception in the West. The "two-for-the-price-of-one" Clintons seemed to exude both philosophies as the campaign took shape, though Hillary immediately flailed at Obama after his injudicious remarks about rural Pennsylvanians clinging to their guns and religion, and looking down on immigrants or minorities.

Obama, one might legitimately argue, was speaking reflexively in terms that far too many Democrats not only understand but quietly endorse. Their elitist attitude about rural Americans has them looking down their noses at people who worship regularly and who own firearms. It is, perhaps, a sad commentary on America that so many young voters have warmed up to the message Obama sends, and the philosophy he seems to share with too many fellow Democrats and party supporters.

That support turned into primary votes in several states as Hillary's campaign hit several speed bumps in the weeks leading up to the Pennsylvania primary, where Obama's comments probably cost him tens of thousands of votes from the rural regions, where people own guns and go to church regularly.

It all translated to delegate votes and primary turnouts that suggested as many people wanted someone other than Hillary as wanted her, and of course, Barack Obama was certainly there to meet their needs and expectations. While the radical Left had earlier embraced Hillary Clinton's liberal extremes, as the campaign wore on, it became clear that Hillary wasn't extreme enough, and younger Democrats – the people Hillary's campaign expected to attract by the legions – had chosen Barack Obama who, while it may not have seemed possible to many conservative and far-right radio talk hosts a couple of years ago, turned out to be even farther to the Left politically than the former First Lady.

But who are these new voters? In a revealing segment of the March 5, 2008 Fox and Friends report in which pollster Frank Luntz quizzed several Ohio college students about why they supported Obama, they could not name a single specific thing he had accomplished as a United States senator. They just liked him because he was, well, *different*. He is certainly younger than Hillary, he appeals to a younger audience, he is a gifted public speaker and he promises "change." Though he was somewhat light on specifics, his "change" message resonated with his younger audiences, for whom "change" has that "grass is greener" appeal, even without knowing whether anything was hiding in the grass.

It created an image of a clueless constituency that had been beguiled by inspiring rhetoric that had nothing to support it.

While Hillary had no great achievements to showcase, despite her claims that she had the "experience" to be commander-in-chief, suddenly it started appear that Obama, like Colorado's famous Platte River, was "a mile wide, but an inch deep." And so were his supporters.

When Republican John McCain had clinched his party's nomination on March 4, 2008 by winning enough delegates during his party's primaries, it appeared at the time that the Democrats would be facing several more weeks of verbal combat between Clinton and Obama. This almost certainly had to be more distressing to Hillary Clinton than others in her party, but for different reasons.

A year earlier, Hillary Clinton had expected to stroll through the primary season as the one true candidate for the true believers. But politics is a contact sport, brutal in nature and cruel in its surprises. In early 2007, one might suggest that Hillary Clinton never even saw Obama coming, or she expected him to be a flash in the pan. In early 2008, not only Hillary but many in the press corps were openly stunned that she had been literally run over by the Obama freight train in eleven straight primary races.

The Acid Test Issue

A funny thing happened on the way to the 2008 election. A clearly volatile right-to-carry issue landed in the spotlight and as a result, the nation got to see whether all the rhetoric about Second Amendment support had any muscle or even sincerity behind it.

And most importantly, it provided an opportunity for pro-gunners to watch two Democrats who had been insisting for months that they "support" the Second Amendment refrain from taking a vote that would reveal them as liars. Some would credibly argue that Clinton and Obama dodged the opportunity to cast another vote on a gun rights issue, which would clearly damage their credibility as supporters of the Second Amendment.

The United States Senate began considering a measure that would change the ways national parks regulate firearms, and would, for the first time, allow American citizens who were legally licensed to carry concealed handguns, bring those loaded guns into parks for their personal protection.

As noted earlier, 51 senators, from both parties, signed a letter to Interior Secretary Dirk Kempthorne – the Interior Department encompasses the National Park Service – to change the rules even without legislation. Gun control organizations, most notably the Brady Campaign to Prevent Gun Violence, were incensed at the effort. They quickly engaged in what author Workman labeled "the politics of hysteria" in a widely-circulated opinion piece, by arguing that passage of the legislation or changing the rules by administrative ruling would "open the parks up to poaching" and more danger to park visitors from stray bullets.

Into this fray stepped Senate Majority Leader Harry Reid of Nevada, who quickly used up any credibility he may ever have had with gun rights activists, when he moved to block a vote on a massive public lands bill to which the concealed carry amendment had been attached. Reid, according to a story carried by the Associated Press and reported in the February 16, 2008 edition of the *Minneapolis Star-Tribune*, was "trying to protect the two leading Democratic candidates for president by shielding them from a politically difficult vote on an issue that many rural voters consider crucial."

Harry Reid was giving his two anti-gun colleagues cover, and the pundits knew it. That may not have made much difference to NBC's horribly partisan Chris Matthews, whose bias toward Obama became clear rather early in the campaign, but it mattered to a lot of gun owners who had been waiting for the opportunity to put both Hillary and Obama in a tight spot, forcing them to stand behind their rhetoric.

Hillary Diane Rodham Clinton and Barack Hussein Obama did not want, nor did either of their campaigns need, a recorded vote on whether armed citizens would be prevented from exercising their right of self-defense and the right to keep and bear arms on federal land. It was a hot-button issue with legions of gun owners who consider a vote on this issue to be the proverbial "acid test" showing whether either Clinton or Obama really "walked the walk" on gun rights, or just "talked the talk."

It did not help matters that Republican nominee Sen. John McCain was a co-sponsor of the concealed carry amendment, which was championed by Sen. Tom Coburn of Oklahoma. That added considerably more weight to the importance of a vote, and Reid, knowing that neither Democrat would support the notion, threw up a roadblock to save them from casting a vote on the Senate floor that would cost one or the other a considerable number of votes at the ballot box in November, depending upon which became the nominee.

Most unusual about the press coverage of this controversy was the blatantly false notion that the measure would open up national wildlife refuges to gun-toting citizens for the purpose of hunting and recreational target shooting. All this demonstrated is that reporters simply cannot get a story right no matter how hard they might try.

National wildlife refuges are already open for hunting, and have been for generations, so people carrying guns on these lands is hardly a novelty. They are not specifically open to the carrying of handguns, though, and the rule change would make that possible. But the refuge system was established during the Theodore Roosevelt administration a century ago, and such refuges have been open to shotgun-toting waterfowl hunters throughout that time.

Reid aides insisted that their boss was not blocking the Coburn measure from consideration to protect the two presidential candidates from having to take an embarrassing vote. That contention wore thin almost immediately, leaving gun owners more convinced than ever that Clinton and Obama were gun control fanatics and had no intention of being nailed down on a gun vote while they were vigorously running against one another for the highest office in the land. And it also convinced gun owners and some political pundits that Reid was giving them cover.

While anti-gunners carried on a largely emotional campaign against guns in parks, the authors obtained data from the National Park Service that revealed that from 2002 through 2006, there had been 63 confirmed homicides in the nation's parks, including the slaying of one armed park ranger. There had been 240 rapes or attempted rapes reported, along with 309 robberies, 37 kidnappings and a whopping 1,277 aggravated assaults.

Of course, stacked against the number of visitors who annually enter our national parks, those numbers constitute an almost microscopic number of offenses. That is true, except for the victims of those crimes, and their families. For them, being victimized inside a national park – with the exception of an animal attack – leaves the horrible, and accurate, impression that despite all claims about parks being among the safest places in the nation, the authorities failed to prevent a crime. Proponents of concealed carry inside national parks contend that, while not everyone will take advantage of a rules change, nor will every intended victim have a firearm, at least that option would exist. Under the ban, no such choice is available, and criminals know it.

In the early 1980s, when then-Interior Secretary James Watt (under President Ronald Reagan) had adopted rules about firearms in parks, only six states had concealed carry statutes on the books. By 2008, there were 40 states with so-called "right-to-carry" laws and another eight with "discretionary" statutes that allowed police to determine who could and could not obtain a carry permit or license.

Traditionally, national forest lands are managed for firearms regulations per the state statutes in which the specific forest is located. Not so with the national parks, and that was the issue at hand. Proponents of the legislative change insisted that national forest lands – which are administered by the Department of Agriculture – and national park lands should have essentially the same regulations for the carrying of concealed firearms for personal protection.

Throughout the controversy, there was no indication from Hillary Clinton or Barack Obama that they understood this issue, or even cared about it, other than perhaps that they knew enough to not want to vote on the measure.

One might offer a credible argument that not only was Harry Reid running interference for Hillary and Barack, so, too, was the Brady Campaign to Prevent Gun Violence by wading into the debate.

Arguments Ignore Facts

Throughout this debate, it was obvious that not only were opponents of the concealed carry proposal ignoring facts about the practice, they were avoiding those facts altogether. This has traditionally been a problem with anti-gun activists and their politician friends, and on one level it seems to be a world class case of denial, while on another level one might justifiably suggest that the gun control movement was in the hands of idiots. In the latter regard, there appears to be much idiocy to go around, since it is always a different bunch of locally-based activists who oppose such laws, but their rhetoric seems to come right out of a playbook filled with the same tired talking points.

In virtually every state where right-to-carry concealed handgun statutes have been adopted over the past 10-15 years, the debate has been generously slathered with anti-self-defense rhetoric that has later proven to be consistently false. Opposition is invariably steeped in emotionalism, virtually bereft of fact.

Occasionally, the sun shines through.

Early in 2008, the *Detroit Free Press* revealed that the Great Lakes State had enjoyed a generally lower violent crime rate during the six years since adopting right-to-carry legislation than it had during the six years prior to the law change. In addition, the incidence of death from suicide and firearms accidents had also dropped. Not surprisingly, when this news broke, gun control proponents were largely silent, and the news media ignored the significance of the revelation.

Had the newspaper reported just the opposite – that crime, suicide and accident rates had gone up since passage of the concealed carry law – one might credibly suggest, based on past performance by the press on the gun issue, that it would have made headlines for days across the country, and would certainly have come up in presidential debates.

Michigan is not the only "success" story ignored by the press and politicians, which explains why the issue does not come up during campaign debates. Neither group knows much about the subject. Generally what they think they know is derived from information they have gotten from gun control groups.

In Texas, for example, as far back as 1999 the authorities knew that all of the dire predictions from self-defense opponents had failed to materialize. According to the National Center for Policy Analysis, using statistics from the Texas Department of Public Safety, between 1995 (the year concealed carry was adopted) and 1999, aggravated assault, robbery, rape and murder all declined.

According to the Center's report, "As a group, Texans with concealed-weapon permits are far less likely to commit crimes than other Texans, says Sterling Burnett of the National Center for Policy Analysis."

The study quoted Burnett, who observed, "You don't get a concealed carry permit because you want to commit a crime (but) because you fear crimes against you."

Benjamin Kepple wrote about this in *Investor's Business Daily* on October 13, 2000, according to the report.

The Wisconsin Policy Research Institute weighed in on the Texas situation – Wisconsin is one of only two remaining states that do not have some form of concealed carry structure – quoting District Attorney John B. Holmes of Harris County, Texas.

"As you know," Holmes stated, "I was very outspoken in my opposition to the passage of the Concealed Handgun Act. I did not feel that such legislation was in the public interest and presented a clear and present danger to law-abiding citizens by placing more handguns on our street. Boy, was I wrong. Our experience in Harris County, and indeed statewide, has proven my initial fears absolutely groundless."

Where this debate leads is to one logical conclusion: legally-armed private citizens who have gone through all of the processes necessary to secure a carry license or permit are not going to jeopardize their gun rights by doing something stupid inside a national park, same as they would not do something foolish anywhere else.

All of this information, and the anecdotal reinforcement, is easily found on the Internet and there would be no reason for anyone in the United States Senate to conclude that concealed carry inside a national park would pose any threat to public safety. Therefore, the only reason to oppose the notion would be because of one's personal dislike for guns, and that's what Harry Reid would want both Clinton and Obama to avoid: having to vote their personal distaste toward firearms and the people who own and carry them. That sort of revelation in a presidential contest can be devastating.

Does avoiding a discussion of this issue by political candidates make them idiots? Hardly. Indeed, in the gun rights community, such people are already considered idiots for ever believing the hysteria in the first place, so it is probably wise for them to remain mute on the issue.

But their silence – when 51 of their colleagues had signed a letter to the Interior secretary seeking a change of park regulations – was deafening, and by blocking a vote on the matter, Reid did neither Clinton nor Obama any favors. Such silence can be irreparably harmful to a political campaign, provided one has any credibility with gun owners to begin with. Since that was never the case with Hillary Clinton or Barack Obama, perhaps the discussion is moot…and Harry Reid did all of that road-blocking for nothing.

Not Biggest Problem

Guns in national parks, and avoiding a vote on the subject, was hardly Hillary Clinton's biggest problem on the campaign trail. It might be logically argued – and it probably will be in the years to come – that Hillary's leisurely stroll down Easy Street to the Democratic nomination ended abruptly over the course of a 90-second exchange in the Autumn of 2007. It was the moment that Hillary Clinton's campaign turned into a hike and ultimately became a daunting climb that failed to reach the summit.

That moment came during her now-infamous "double-back-flip" on live television in the October 30, 2007 debate at Drexel University in Philadelphia when she was up against six opponents and made the remarkably foolish error of defending the idea of issuing driver's licenses to illegal aliens, which was being championed at the time by then-New York Gov. Eliot Spitzer, and then insisting that she "did not say that it should be done."

(Spitzer was less than six months away from seeing his career self-destruct when his long-term involvement with a prostitution ring was revealed.)

That was when NBC's Tim Russert, who was sitting on the panel of moderators, fired back at the former First Lady, reminding her, "You told (a) New Hampshire paper that it made a lot of sense. Do you support his plan?"

And instead of a straight "yes" or "no" answer, Hillary's defenses visibly came up and she told Russert, "You know, Tim, this is where everybody plays 'gotcha'."

It was a watershed moment in Hillary's campaign, and perhaps her career, as the entire country suddenly saw what happens when you back her into a corner. As reporter Roger Simon wrote the following day in *The Politico*, "It was not that her answer about whether illegal immigrants should be issued driver's licenses was at best incomprehensible and at worst misleading.

"It was that for two hours, she dodged and weaved, parsed and stonewalled."

"And when it was over," Simon observed, "both the Barack Obama and John Edwards campaigns signaled that in the weeks ahead they intend to hammer home a simple message: Hillary Clinton does not say what she means or mean what she says."

That message resonated from one end of the nation to the other, and as the primary season unfolded, Hillary's string of losses to Obama could well have been triggered by the October debacle. The once invincible candidate now became very vulnerable.

If Hillary Clinton was already known as the "dog who don't hunt" among gun rights activists, that impression spread rapidly among people for whom firearms ownership is not nearly an important subject as illegal immigration. Once that dent was pounded into Hillary's armor, her opponents came out with sledge hammers.

Where her policies and votes have consistently failed the "acid test" with this nation's gun owners, her performance that night in October 2007 and her portrayal as, which became an image of, a politician who cannot stick to one position from one day, nay one moment, to the next, tainted her campaign far more corrosively, and as it turned out, fatally.

Like it or not, what former Obama aide Samantha Power said about Hillary Clinton being "a monster" that is "stooping to anything" had some adhesive to it, and it stuck. Perhaps the reason it had sticking power is because many American citizens, whether they admit it or not, have long harbored the feeling that Hillary has a dark side.

For example, the circulation of a photo of Obama in a turban and native costume was almost immediately thought to be the handiwork of Clinton campaign operatives, despite loud and emphatic denials. Obama, trying to "remain above the fray" and appear magnanimous, told reporters several days later that he accepted Senator Clinton's word that she was not responsible for circulating that photo to – as he had asserted in late February 2008 when the image first surfaced – "When in the midst of a campaign you decide to throw the kitchen sink at your opponent because you're behind, and you start, your campaign starts leaking photos of me when I'm traveling overseas wearing native clothes of those folks, to make people afraid, then you run an ad talking about who's going to answer the phone at three in the morning, an ad straight out of the Republican playbook, that's not real change. That's not real change. That's the same old thing."

When her campaign was going into melt-down prior to the Texas (where she won the primary but Obama won the caucus and actually came up a few delegates ahead of Clinton) and Ohio primaries, there were reports out of the Clinton campaign that Hillary had gone into rages over her poor showing. That's a far cry from the way Simon described her performance at October 30, 2007 debate, when he wrote, "All of her opponents seemed passionate about one issue or another. But Clinton seemed largely emotionless and detached, often just mouthing rehearsed answers from her briefing book."

All of this came down to a question for voters, whether they voted solely on the gun rights issue, or something else including illegal immigration, health care reform or any number of other causes.

"If Hillary Clinton is elected president, which version of Hillary would occupy the Oval Office," they wondered?

She almost assuredly would have become a gun grabber's gun grabber, if past performance and voting record are any indication, despite any lip service she had given to the Second Amendment along the way. Of that, activists in the gun rights community all the way up to the national organizations including the National Rifle Association, Citizens Committee for the Right to Keep and Bear Arms and Gun Owners of America are unanimously certain.

Hillary can claim the contrary all she wants because the firearms community will simply point to the speed with which she flip-flops on issues as she did during the October 2007 Drexel University debate. If she was that fast on the subject of driver's licenses for illegal immigrants, just how quick would she reverse any public position on gun control?

Besides, when one takes a dispassionate look at what Hillary had been saying through the campaign, she has consistently stated that she "supports the Second Amendment....but." It's at the word "but" where gun owners start holding their collective noses. From that point, her explanations get a little generic, in the same vein as her remarks about issues during the October 2007 debate. There is room, she will say, for "reasonable controls." But that's where it ends. She offers no specifics other than to endorse a renewal of the abysmally failed ban on so-called "assault weapons," because to do so would not simply open the genie's bottle, it would smash the vessel beyond repair.

In fairness, as mentioned earlier, Barack Obama is no better on the issue and in some cases much worse. His website panders that "He will protect the rights of hunters and other law-abiding Americans to purchase, own, transport, and use guns for the purposes of hunting and target shooting," without mentioning a single word about self-defense or resisting government tyranny, the primary reasons for which the specific protection of the right to keep and bear arms was included in the Bill of Rights by the Founders.

Consider the remarks of a genuine woman president about the would-be woman president. Sandra Froman, an attorney in Tucson, Arizona and past president of the National Rifle Association wrote in her on-line column at

TownHall.com that Hillary "does not even pretend to be friendly to America's gun owners."

"She's a Northeastern liberal with a socialist philosophy," Froman wrote on September 29, 2007, "no background or experience with firearms, and fiercely opposes Second Amendment rights. She hates guns, plain and simple. And she doesn't think much of those of us who value our constitutional right to own them."

This broadside came two days after *New York Sun* columnist Ken Blackwell, chairman of the Coalition for a Conservative Majority, sent a barrage across Clinton's bow. In a blistering analysis of the presidential contenders at that point, Blackwell observed, "All the Republican candidates are aware that Hillary Clinton is the most anti-gun candidate ever. Yes, she's to the left of Walter Mondale and George McGovern on guns. She cannot do what Al Gore or John Kerry did, trying to suddenly appear to be hunters and outdoorsmen."

Of course, Blackwell wrote that before Hillary's famous duck hunting recollection surfaced.

And therein lays the key to the discomfort many Americans still feel toward Hillary Diane Rodham Clinton. What they see is on the surface, from a banded duck hunting story to that annoying laugh (some would call it a "cackle") that comes out when she is trying to appear "more human" appears to be far different than what lies beneath the senator's armor.

The fear remains that if ever this woman were ever to somehow ascend to the presidency, the real Hillary Clinton will eventually emerge from beneath the façade.

Eight

THE RACE (CARD) IS ON

American gun owners have been traditionally and viciously stereotyped by anti-gun lobbyists, writers and editorial cartoonists as ignorant beer-bellied rednecks that are careless with firearms, and may have a racist streak that runs wide and deep.

It is a stereotype invented by the liberal Left for its own purposes, not the least of which is to smear and demonize its opponents and critics, and as the events of the 2008 Democratic primary revealed – while liberal commentators and even reporters attempted to gloss over the facts – it is a portrayal that may have been created to camouflage the very real, and inherently racist attitudes harbored by the very same Left.

After all, gun rights activists can readily explain, American gun control laws are deeply rooted in racism, and the party that championed those laws was the Democrats. To fully understand this colossal hypocrisy, one must first put this covert racism in perspective.

From Bill Clinton's references toward African-American voters in South Carolina to the monumental gaffe by former Democratic vice presidential candidate and noted anti-gunner Geraldine Ferraro that led to her departure as Hillary Clinton's chief financial advisor – suggesting that Barack Obama would never have gotten so far as he did in the race had he not been black, observing "If Obama was a white man, he would not be in this position" – the proverbial race card has proved itself to be a "One-Eyed Jack" that only showed one side of its face because the other is simply too ugly for Democrats in denial to accept. And it has been argued with considerable merit that the Democratic Party is in a constant state of denial.

The genuine chasm that exists between white and black Democratic voters began rearing its head in South Carolina, Texas and Mississippi, and festered with the rantings of Rev. Jeremiah Writght and Father Michael Pfleger. Even Bill CLinton contributed to the problem by simply not keeping his mouth shut.

Months after his initial foot-in-mouth remarks about Barack Obama following the South Carolina primary, he was back at it again during an interview with Philadelphia radio station WHYY. His remarks were quoted by Newsmax.com.

The former president accused Obama and his campaign of playing "the race card on me." The following day he denied to reporters in Pittsburgh that he had said it, claiming instead that his remarks were "mischaracterized."

But according to Newsmax.com's report, Clinton told WHYY, "I think that they (the Obama campaign) played the race card on me. And we now know, from memos from the campaign and everything, that they planned to do it all along."

And then, with the interview concluded but the microphone still on, according to Newsmax, Clinton displayed a nasty bit of temper by remarking, "I don't think I should take any s(expletive) from anybody on that, do you?"

Race is an issue that must be confronted as much as the party's egregious historical support for restrictive gun control measures while its members insist they "really do support the Second Amendment" (provided, of course, that they can regulate it into irrelevance).

As Barack Obama continually preached through his campaign that it is "time for change," perhaps it is also time for the Democrat Party to confront the racism within its own ranks. Bounce this off leaders in the party, and they will strenuously deny such racism exists; after all, they are the self-appointed (self-anointed?) "progressive" party, and everyone knows racists can only be conservative white people who own guns, or so the Left would have us believe.

Then came press disclosures, complete with video as proof, about the outbursts of Obama's own pastor in Chicago, the afrementioned fiery Rev. Jeremiah Wright Jr. of the Trinity United Church of Christ in which he criticized Hillary Clinton and excoriated the United States, claiming that "we started the AIDS virus" and lamenting that "Barack knows what it means living in a country and a culture that is controlled by rich white people. Hillary would never know that."

Perhaps not coincidentally, leaping to the defense of the Rev. Wright was that other Chicago-area clergyman, Catholic priest Michael Pfleger. This is the man who has spearheaded a campaign against gun ownership since his adopted son was gunned down in 1998 by a killer who has never been caught. Pfleger told one of the authors in an interview that he is far less interested in catching criminals, including the person who gunned down his adopted son, than he is in removing firearms from society.

Pfleger, along with the Rev. Jesse Jackson, was arrested for trespassing in the summer of 2007 during a demonstration in front of Chuck's Gun Shop in Riverside, Illinois, a Chicago suburb. This was a couple of weeks after Pfleger, during a speech to a crowd of gun control supporters, had suggested pulling gun shop owner John Riggio out of Chuck's and "snuffing" him. "Snuff' is a slang term for kill. The Chicago Archdiocese was less than pleased with Pfleger, who has acknowledged that he is "very, very anti-gun."

This might explain why Pfleger tried to downplay the Rev. Wright's remarks, claiming to not fully realize what the term "snuff" meant to someone else. And then the video of Pfleger's own racist rant about Hillary surfaced.

Pfleger has told his own parishioners, "If you're not a law enforcement officer you should not have a gun in your house."

Pfleger's bigotry against guns and the people who own them, and his defense of Wright's incendiary orations that included the recommendation to his congregation that instead of singing "God Bless America" they should be saying "God Damn America" only reinforce the notion that the Left firmly believes the ends justify the means. Such remarks are hardly dismissible as the rantings of extremists on the fringe, and only because so many who consider themselves in the "mainstream" are quick to offer defenses or lame excuses for this kind of behavior. They may be extremists, but there are serious concerns and sensible arguments that they represent the core leadership philosophy of the party, not the "fringe." Indeed, they are hardly alone on the Far Left with their philosophies, and the Far Left has been steering the Democrat Party for years.

And let us not forget Jesse Jackson, a perennial anti-gunner and one-time Democratic candidate for the presidency. Jackson is also a habitual publicity seeker who has been criticized for "never letting facts get between him and a camera."

Always one to try for the clever sound bite, Jackson issued a press release when he demonstrated with Pfleger, in which Jackson stated, "Our marching does not kill people; people who buy guns from gun shops kill people." Law-abiding citizens buy firearms at gun shops, criminals typically do not, because a gun shop retail purchase involves a federal background check. Jackson knows this. He was simply trying to demonize firearms retailers like Riggio, and his customers, who are largely members of minority groups.

Racism and gun laws

How odd and ironic that the Democrats would traditionally preach gun control and attack what they claim is racism among conservatives, when there is ample historic evidence that the first gun laws were designed specifically to prevent freed Southern blacks from being able to arm themselves against the abuses of white night riders. Those laws were championed by Democrats.

In his remarkable essay *Gun Control and Racism*, published in the *George Mason University Civil Rights Law Journal* (Vol. 2, 1991), Stefan B. Tahmassebi, then an assistant general counsel for the National Rifle Association (and now its deputy general counsel), detailed the sinister roots of gun control in America. While it should be required reading for law students, civil rights attorneys (especially those at the American Civil Liberties Union), all Democrats on Capitol Hill and in state legislatures from coast to coast, the Far Left has hidden within its state of denial and failed to confront this terrible history.

Noted Tahmassebi in his introduction: "The history of gun control in America possesses an ugly component: discrimination and oppression of blacks, other racial and ethnic minorities, immigrants, and other 'unwanted elements,' including union organizers and agrarian reformers. Firearms laws were often enacted to disarm and facilitate repressive action against these groups."

He further explained that the first gun control laws in the nation were "enacted in the ante-bellum South forbidding blacks, whether free or slave, to possess arms, in order to maintain blacks in their servile status." Tahmassebi's essay should be required reading in every high school American history class in the nation.

In the post-Civil War South during Reconstruction, southern legislatures were dominated by Democrats, who had championed secession following the 1860 election of Republican Abraham Lincoln as president. Everyone remembers Lincoln as the man who issued the Emancipation Proclamation, but far too many Americans have forgotten which political party he belonged to. Southerners saw Republicans as the party of northern aggression, so when the war was over, it was Democrats who quickly regained control in the South, championing so-called "Black Codes" which, among other things, were engineered to keep blacks disarmed.

According to a brief historical look the post-Civil War Democrat politics in the South on Wikipedia, by the election of 1870, the Democrat party was able to gain control of Congress, bringing an end to Republican-led Reconstruction. Democrats in the South adhered to the states rights issue up through the 1960s. Alabama's segregationist Gov. George Wallace was a Democrat, as was Arkansas Gov. Orval Faubus – the man who used the National Guard to enforce segregation in Little Rock and prevent black children from attending a high school there – and the national party has never apologized but has certainly endeavored to sweep under the rug the opposition Southern Democrats mounted to the Civil Rights Act.

As detailed by the Dirksen Congressional Center's on-line discussion of the debate over the Civil Rights Act, headlined Major Features of the Civil Rights Act of 1964, it was Democrats who were essentially split over the issue, not Republicans. The article notes that in the House of Representatives, "Republicans favored the bill 138 to 34; Democrats supported it 152-96. It is interesting to note that Democrats from northern states voted overwhelmingly for the bill, 141 to 4, while Democrats from southern states voted overwhelmingly against the bill, 92 to 11."

When the bill reached the Senate, the Dirksen Center's history detailed, "Only one Republican senator participated in the filibuster against the bill. In fact, since 1933, Republicans had a more positive record on civil rights than the Democrats. In the twenty-six major civil rights votes since 1933, a majority of Democrats opposed civil rights legislation in over 80% of the votes. By contrast, the Republican majority favored civil rights in over 96% of the votes."

Is it not ironic that while the Democratic party has, over the past four decades, portrayed itself as a champion of civil rights, the party has steadfastly supported ever increasing restrictions on one important civil right: the Right to Keep and Bear Arms?

But it has not just been Democrats in the South who championed gun control laws that were racially and politically motivated. In New York, the infamous Sullivan Law was the brainchild of Timothy D. "Big Tim" Sullivan, a key figure in the Tammany Hall Democratic machine of the early 1900s.

The foundation for this insidious gun law was to prevent immigrants from southern Europe, primarily Italians, from legally owning firearms, specifically handguns. As Tahmassebi noted in his essay, "The fear and suspicion of these 'undesirable' immigrants, together with a desire to disarm labor organizers, led to a concerted campaign by local and national business associations and organizations such as the Immigration Restriction League and the American Protective Association, for the enactment of a flat ban on the ownership of firearms, or at least handguns, by aliens."

The Sullivan Law, he explained, made it impossible for anyone to legally own a gun without a permit from the New York Police Department, which was squarely in the control of Sullivan and the Tammany Hall bosses. Then, as today, essentially only the elite and politically connected can get a permit in the City of New York, while average citizens simply do not enjoy the same ability.

Tahmassebi recalled that the police began cancelling pistol permits in the Italian sections of the city "as early as 1903."

"This was followed by a state law of 1905 which made it illegal for aliens to possess firearms 'in any public place'," he wrote. "This provision was retained in the Sullivan law."

The Sullivan Law was passed in 1911 and remains as one of the nation's toughest and perhaps most Draconian gun laws today, and Democrats including Hillary Clinton and Barack Obama have suggested that this is the kind of "reasonable" gun control law they support, in spite of their verbal "support for the Second Amendment."

Tahmassebi's superb overview of the history of gun control in this country includes a rather telling, if not outright alarming, summation of what gun control efforts have really been designed for.

"During the later part of the 19th century and the early part of the 20th century," he observed, "gun control laws were passed in the South in order to disarm agrarian reformers and in the North to disarm union organizers. In the North, a strong xenophobic reaction to recent waves of immigrants added further fuel for gun control laws which were used to disarm such persons. Other firearms ownership restrictions were adopted in order to repress the incipient black civil rights movement."

Gun control spreads

While Democrats have a rather soiled history when it comes to championing and passing gun control laws, conservatives have no small amount of soiled laundry in their own right, as Tahmassebi noted in his lengthy essay.

"Conservative business associations," he recalled, "through a nationwide handgun prohibition campaign endorsing the Sullivan-type law concept, were responsible for enacting police permit requirements in Arkansas, Hawaii, Michigan, Missouri, New Jersey, North Carolina and Oregon, between 1911 and 1934. The then conservative institutions of the *New York Times* and the American Bar Association supported this campaign. By fueling a spreading fear of armed robbery, these business interests were able to push for restrictive gun laws that were really aimed at the disarmament of labor organizations and agrarian agitators."

Arkansas, Michigan, Missouri, North Carolina and Oregon lawmakers, pressed by their law-abiding constituents to do so, have joined scores of other states in adopting firearms-friendly statutes that have recognized and expanded concealed carry laws. The *New York Times* and American Bar Association, on the other hand, have hardly turned over a new political leaf on the subject of gun rights. The newspaper particularly has a long tradition of editorial tirades against gun ownership, and it has a staff of reporters who continually write about guns as though they are bereft of even the most fundamental knowledge of firearms.

While it would be foolish to suggest some "vast Left Wing conspiracy" exists among today's press to shield anti-gun Democrats from negative publicity, gun rights is hardly an issue that reporters and editors care to use to challenge the views of Democrats running for political office. The issue has been kept on the back burner, if not on the warmer, with coverage limited to perhaps a few paragraphs here and there in the reams of news columns generated by the 2008 presidential campaign.

That was one reason why gun rights groups waited with great anticipation and high expectations as the Supreme Court considered a court challenge to the District of Columbia's handgun ban.

And herein lies part of the problem for Democrats: While they have "danced around" the challenge to define specifically what they believe a "reasonable firearms regulation" might encompass, they have indicated support for local laws that require registration, licensing, waiting periods or a ban as imposed by the District of Columbia metropolitan government for more than 30 years. Gun owners are not nearly as gullible as Left-liberal Democrats think they are, and to suggest that tight restrictions or outright bans are "reasonable" insults their intelligence.

If there is one lesson Democrats never seem to learn despite all of the political losses they suffer as a result, it is that firearms owners, and particularly gun rights activists, are not the fools Democrats take them for.

Yes, it can be argued that Republicans became a disappointment for gun owners during the late 1990s and first years of the second Bush Administration for not living up to the promise they represented, the Democrats as a party have, for the past few decades, essentially treated this nation's gun owners as second class citizens not to be trusted with the exercise of a fundamental civil right. This outrage has been exacerbated by Democrats who support increasingly restrictive gun laws, then ask gun owners, "What? What did I do?" as if they had no notion their actions would enrage their gun owning constituents.

This brings us back around to Hillary Diane Rodham Clinton; in her case lies the text book example of how gun owners will remember those who historically have hurt them and voted against their interests. Hillary can insist forcefully that she "supports the Second Amendment," but she has a track record that convinces the firearms community that this is simply not true. That which is not true is a lie, and gun owners understand very well when they have been lied to repeatedly, and when they have been wronged consistently, and they have rather long memories.

And let us not overlook Barack Obama, who does not have as extensive a track record on gun control votes as Clinton, but who has taken positions that offend and alarm gun owners. As Second Amendment authority David Kopel wrote in the *Wall Street Journal* on April 17, 2008, "When the U.S. Supreme Court voted last year to hear a case on the constitutionality of the Washington, D.C., handgun ban, Mr. Obama's campaign told the Chicago Tribune: 'Obama believes the D.C. handgun law is constitutional' and that 'local communities' should have the ability 'to enact common sense laws.'...As a state senator, Mr. Obama voted against a 2004 bill (which passed overwhelmingly) to give citizens a legal defense against prosecution for violating a local handgun ban if they actually used the firearm for lawful self-defense on their own property.

"Mr. Obama's campaign Web site touts his belief in the Second Amendment rights to have guns 'for the purposes of hunting and target shooting'," Kopel added. "Conspicuously absent is the right to have firearms to defend one's self, home and family. In 2001, as a state senator, Mr. Obama voted against allowing the beneficiaries of domestic violence protective orders to carry handguns for protection."

It is perhaps not surprising that the Liberal Left, including the so-called "mainstream press," has consistently failed to acknowledge that gun owners, and especially gun rights activists, have a keen understanding of, and appreciation for, the racist history of gun control laws in this country, yet here in the vanguard against gun rights is Barack Obama. The press and the Liberal Left simply believe their invented stereotypes, and they refuse to accept the fact that the gun-owners they consider Neanderthals actually have a solid grasp of, and are disgusted by, the racist foundation of gun control laws. Gun owners understand – while Democrats continue to deny – that those laws have also been instituted and enforced to separate the classes. Indeed, the firearms community has a far better understanding of the origins of the gun control movement in this nation than those who champion that cause.

The anti-gun Left which dominates the Democratic Party hides behind its arrogance and wallows in the self-delusion that liberals can't be racists or bigots, when in reality, they can be among the worst.

The people who most strenuously promote various gun laws, up to and including outright bans on certain types of firearms and who staunchly approved of the handgun ban in the District of Columbia are the same people who steadfastly refuse to admit the racist history of the Democratic Party and how it has historically conducted class warfare in America, with the attack on gun rights being a cornerstone of that war. Perhaps the greatest irony of all is that many of the proponents of such race-based laws are themselves members of minority ethnic groups.

In addition to Barack Obama, Washington, D.C. Mayor Adrian Fenty and New Orleans Mayor Ray Nagin are African-American, as are Rep. Charles Rangel (D-NY), Eleanor Holmes Norton (District of Columbia delegate to Congress), Jesse Jackson, and Rep. Melvin Watt of North Carolina. All of these people are strongly anti-gun and every one of them is a Democrat.

The politics of division

One wonders why it must be that a political party and those who step forward to represent its values at times seem more interested in divisiveness than unity.

In the case of the Democrat Left adopting the elitist philosophy that gun owners are somehow less sophisticated, intelligent, urbane or capable of making their own choices, the Democrats have often become what they claim to despise the most: bigots. This is reflected almost on a daily basis somewhere in America, when Liberals are identified as "progressives." While it is not explained, the subtle message not spoken is that those of another persuasion, who may disagree with policies and politics of the Liberal agenda – the Democrat agenda – are somehow regressive. And with that, we're right back to comparing these individuals to Neanderthals because they do not conform, therefore, they are "not enlightened."

From the party that wanted to keep Reconstruction era blacks disarmed to the party that wants to keep everybody (except, perhaps, privileged elitists like themselves, plus the police and military) disarmed – and critics will defensively call this a crass and overly broad generalization – Democrats have, as Desi Arnaz would tell Lucille Ball on their 1950's sitcom "a lot of 'splainin' to do."

But they dodge the explanation, perhaps because they realize there is no acceptable explanation to be offered. So, they deflect the issue and move to a more comfortable conversation.

Anti-gun Democrats have adopted a strategy that changes their rhetoric, but not necessarily their ultimate goals. They carefully craft their message to include such terms as "sensible gun safety" and "reasonable regulation." But for some people, "reasonable regulation" translates to the authority to ban guns.

Firearms owners often feel as though they are being treated as second-class citizens. Gun rights activists have occasionally noted that gun owners, as a social group, are the only people in America against whom it is still fashionable to practice social bigotry.

Law-abiding gun owners, for example, are prohibited from carrying firearms in certain places (and those places will vary from state to state), even though people licensed to carry concealed guns have gone through background checks. How would members of the Liberal Left react if suddenly they were prohibited from entering certain buildings or public parks?

In some states, gun owners are prohibited from carrying their guns into public buildings, or public places such as theaters, shopping malls, schools, hospitals or restaurants even though there is no evidence that legally-armed citizens have ever posed a public threat. But the hysteria created by gun control advocates and used to fuel anti-gun legislation authored consistently by Democrats has left a large segment of the American public distrustful of any fellow citizen who chooses to exercise his or her constitutional right to keep and bear arms. Gun owners are viewed with suspicion, and so city and county governments, and state legislatures continue to incrementally erode their gun rights with one limitation on top of another.

All of these measures against law-abiding gun owners are a manifestation of what the late actor Charlton Heston, who served an unprecedented five years as president of the National Rifle Association, called a "cultural war." In a speech at Brandeis University on March 28, 2000, Heston clearly defined this cultural war by observing, "More and more we are fueled by anger, a fury fed by those who profit from it. Democrats hate Republicans. Gays hate straights. Women hate men. Liberals hate conservatives. Vegetarians hate meat eaters. Gun banners hate gun owners.

"Politicians, the media, even the entertainment industry is keenly aware that heated controversy wins votes, snares ratings and keeps the box office humming," Heston added. "They are experts at dangling the bait, and Americans are eager to rise to it...As a result, we are becoming increasingly fragmented as a people. Our one nation, under God, with liberty and justice for all now seems more like the fractured streets of Beirut, echoing with anger."

Heston carried his message about the cultural war being waged against gun owners to many audiences, from college students to the Washington, D.C. press corps when he spoke to the National Press Club on February 11, 1997.

Did his words change anything? Probably not within the extreme Left, because the war against gun owners is still being waged and it is deeply rooted in the Democrat foundation whether it is an official plank in the party platform or not. This divisiveness is what attracts many on the Far Left to the Democratic Party, for they find themselves among their soulmates. Unfortunately for the Democratic Party, the political leaders of this cultural war remain at the party's helm, and two with the most vehemently anti-gun records are the ones who rose to the top after the various Democratic presidential primaries, while the only one with even a moderately pro-gun record, New Mexico Gov. Bill Richardson, was a distant also-ran.

But Heston did wake up Americans in the middle to what he believed was, and remains, an insidious threat to the future of a nation he loved. Heston saw the attacks on the Second Amendment as the proverbial camel's nose under the tent; a symptom of an even deeper threat.

Clear evidence of this might exist in the now infamous remarks of Barack Obama to people at a private fund-raiser in San Francisco in early April 2008 when he commented that "it's not surprising then (rural Pennsylvanians) get bitter, they cling to guns or religion or antipathy to people who aren't like them or anti-immigrant sentiment or anti-trade sentiment as a way to explain their frustrations."

Translation: Those rural gun-owning hicks who go to church and believe in God take out their frustrations about unemployment and other problems on illegal immigrants. "They're not sophisticated and 'progressive,' like us."

To her credit as a politician more than someone who may actually believe her own rhetoric, Hillary Clinton was quick to seize on this insulting remark and make it an issue (though a press corps that fawns over Obama was just as quick in its effort to downplay and ultimately sweep under the rug Obama's comments).

Hillary correctly called Obama's remarks "elitist and divisive." She delivered a speech that included this reminder to Obama, and any of his supporters who shared his elitist notion: "People enjoy hunting and shooting because it's an important part of who they are, not because they are bitter."

Quoted by ABC News, she told reporters in Scranton, PA on April 13, 2008, "I do not believe, as Senator Obama apparently does, that Americans in small towns and small cities and rural areas cling to religion and gun ownership out of frustration they embrace them as a matter of faith and a way of life. We are at a point in America where need to be bringing people together."

If only Hillary's Democrat colleagues actually believed that.

Nine

HILLARY WANTS A 'GUN SUMMIT'

Firearms rights versus gun control; toss that subject into a room filled with political activists and politicians, and you will either see people running for the door or rolling up their sleeves to argue.

Like any Democrat, Hillary Diane Rodham Clinton knows the subject of guns is a hot-button that is begging to be pressed and she does not want anyone's finger on that particular trigger unless she can control the discussion. Democrats who lost their seats in Congress in November 1994 know all too well that the wrong position on gun rights can bring down the wrath of voters who cast their ballots on a single issue.

However, during a question-and-answer session on the campaign trail in DePere, Wisconsin in February 2008, Hillary told the audience that she favors holding a "presidential summit on gun control," according to a commentary that appeared in the February 18 issue of the New York Daily News. This was, the newspaper noted, in reaction to a question from a woman about the then-recent shooting at Northern Illinois University.

What kind of a summit would this be? According to Hillary, it would be a event "where everybody comes together on all sides of this issue."

"Let's figure out how we can be consistent with the Second Amendment," she said, "which I wholeheartedly support, and do more to keep people safe.

"I think we can do that," she continued, "but it's going to require us all to maybe give a little and understand the point of view of the other people."

Yeah, like that would ever really happen, especially under a Hillary Clinton or Barack Obama presidency.

Put, for example, Larry Pratt, head of the Gun Owners of America in the same room with Josh Sugarmann from the Violence Policy Center, and you will be lucky to get them to agree on the sanctity of motherhood. Pratt might start the debate maintaining that gun owners have already "given a lot, not a little" and gotten nothing in return. Sugarmann might say that gun owners haven't given up enough, and that they must agree to surrender their handguns, all semi-auto rifles and shotguns, and register so-called "sniper rifles," that is, any hunting rifle equipped with a riflescope, which are today as common as sport-utility vehicles.

And Hillary, as president, would have brought these people together for a little "give-and-take?" Civil discourse would cease immediately and the summit would descend into little more than a shouting match.

Here is a senator from New York who would not, presumably for political expediency, take a position by signing either of two documents sent to the Supreme Court in the case of *District of Columbia v. Heller,* one from 51 of her colleagues and Vice President Dick Cheney asking the court to affirm that the Second Amendment protects and individual civil right, and the other from 17 members of the House of Representatives that asked the court uphold the city's 32-year-old handgun ban.

This is one of only 16 United States senators to vote against a measure that would prohibit authorities from confiscating firearms from law-abiding citizens in the wake of a natural or man-made disaster, without warrant or probable cause. (It should come as no surprise that all 16 were Democrats: Daniel Akaka and Daniel Inouye, Hawaii; Barbara Boxer and Dianne Feinstein, California; Frank Lautenberg and Robert Menendez of New Jersey; Barbara Mikulski and Paul Sarbanes, Maryland; Richard Durbin, Illinois; Edward M. Kennedy, Massachusetts; Carl Levin, Michigan; Christopher Dodd, Connecticut; Tom Harkin, Iowa; Jack Reed, Rhode Island, plus New York's Charles Schumer, and Hillary Clinton.)

She is a senator with a long track record of being in favor of every gun control bill that came to her attention, and who miraculously shifts gears during the presidential campaign to declare that she "supports the Second Amendment...but."

She is the former First Lady who initially ran for the senate seat vacated by Daniel Patrick Moynihan, and a cornerstone of her campaign in 2000 was gun control.

Hillary Diane Rodham Clinton is the woman who would have brought all sides together under one roof to discuss this issue in a rational atmosphere, presumably without taking sides? Good luck on that.

This notion does, perhaps, signify to gun-owning voters that Hillary Clinton apparently believes they have short or cloudy memories. She would be disappointed to know that the 4 million members of the National Rifle Association have hardly forgotten her activities post-Columbine High School in 1999. The Citizens Committee for the Right to Keep and Bear Arms has vivid memories of Hillary Clinton advocating licensing for gun owners and registration of their firearms as part of a "comprehensive plan" to combat violent crime in which firearms are used. Gun Owners of America keeps scrupulous details of her voting record on their website.

She has insisted that she has "backed off" those plans and that earlier

91

rhetoric. But gun owners remember what Bill Clinton said in 1990 about not being in favor of gun control and during the first two years of his presidency he signed two pieces of legislation that infuriated and insulted the firearms community. Those same gun owners also recall that when Bill was running hard for the presidency, the campaign made much of that "two-for-the-price-of-one" arrangement that many saw as putting Hillary in the White House as an unelected co-president who became something of a champion of gun control legislation.

According to *New York Daily News* writer Michael McAuliff, who wrote the short piece about Hillary's desire for a gun summit, she observed that "We know we need better background checks and we know we've got to have mental health information in there."

That's one side of a "back-and-forth" that Hillary evidently envisions. On the other side are issues about restoration of firearms rights for people convicted of certain crimes, or protection of gun rights for people who have not been convicted of any crime, but are subject to protection orders that may have been unjustly filed as a leverage ploy in a divorce proceeding.

There might also be suggestions relating to nationwide recognition of concealed carry permits, and legislation to either rein in the Bureau of Alcohol, Tobacco, Firearms and Explosives, or abolish the agency altogether.

The problem, as detailed by gun rights advocates in the past, has been that historically whenever gun control proponents want to sit down and negotiate, they bring nothing to the table but a wish list of concessions they want from the firearms community. "Gun grabbers," as they have been labeled by John Snyder with the Citizens Committee for the Right to Keep and Bear Arms, have never once proposed a gun control measure by offering something in exchange for whatever it was they expected gun owners to give up. They couch their demands in emotion-laden rhetoric about child safety and "gun violence."

So, when Hillary Clinton starts talking about "give-and-take," the firearms community justifiably argues that this translates into "You give, and we'll take."

Turning back the clock

In the Nevada candidates debate, Hillary told the audience that "we need to enforce the (gun) laws we have on the books."

As recalled by ABC's Jake Tapper, she also stated, "I would also work to reinstate the assault-weapons ban."

That's failing the acid test the easy way, ironically while repeating the rhetoric of the National Rifle Association, which has for years insisted that enforcement of existing gun laws will have a far greater impact on crime than simply writing new laws, and that includes renewing a ban that was the showpiece of the anti-gun movement.

But there is a problem with the ban that few people outside the gun community care to discuss. For the ten years it was in effect, the ban on so-called "assault weapons" (which was not really a ban at all, but a prohibition on new manufacture and import of certain semiautomatic firearms with specific design features and their full-capacity magazines) had no significant impact on the crime rates.

Professor John Lott, one of the nation's preeminent authorities on firearms crime data and the effect of gun laws on violent crime rates, revealed in an essay published on June 29, 2005 – nine months after the ban sunsetted – that murders in the United States declined *after* the ban ended.

"Even more interesting," Lott wrote, "the seven states that have their own assault weapons bans saw a smaller drop in murders than the 43 states without such laws, suggesting that doing away with the ban actually reduced crime. (States with bans averaged a 2.4% decline in murders; in three states with bans, the number of murders rose. States without bans saw murders fall by more than 4%.)"

Lott pulled no punches in that article, recalling that leading gun control activist Sarah Brady, for whose husband the 1993 Brady Law was named, had predicted hysterically that if the ban were allowed to sunset, "our streets are going to be filled with AK-47s and Uzis." Murder rates would skyrocket, she intimated, and the streets would become bloody battlegrounds.

It did not happen that way. According to Lott, who wrote, "The fact that the end of the assault weapons ban didn't create a crime wave should not have surprised anyone. After all, there is not a single published academic study showing that these bans have reduced any type of violent crime.

"Research funded by the Justice Department under the Clinton administration concluded only that the effect of the assault weapons ban on gun violence 'has been uncertain'," Lott reported. "The authors of that report released their updated findings last August (2003), looking at crime data from 1982 through 2000 (which covered the first six years of the federal law). The latest version stated: 'We cannot clearly credit the ban with any of the nation's recent drop in gun violence'."

This Justice Department study was launched during the Clinton Administration – when Hillary was still part of the "two-for-the-price-of-one" team – and it concluded that a drop in crime during the latter days of that administration could not be linked to the ban. Surely Hillary is aware of this report, and yet she clings to the notion that banning so-called "assault weapons" will somehow address the problem of violent crime.

Why does Hillary want to reinstate a ban on certain types of firearms that is known to have not accomplished what it was supposed to?

It is because the gun control movement revolves around symbolism rather than substance, and its ultimate goal is to ban private firearms ownership.

The only way to accomplish that is to first make it publicly acceptable to ban certain types of firearms, based on their appearance or magazine capacity or a combination of components. This erosion of firearms ownership is a gradual thing, and what is most astounding is that, while gun control legislation infuriates millions of gun owners and affects tens of millions of law-abiding American citizens, rarely does one see these same citizens exert the political power they would possess as a voting bloc.

It has happened, of course, with the change of Congress in the 1994 elections, the loss by Al Gore of three key states including his own during the 2000 presidential election that gave George Bush the White House, and in state-level elections. Massachusetts voters soundly rejected an initiative to ban handguns in 1976. California voters defeated Proposition 15, the statewide freeze on handgun registration in 1982. Washington state voters crushed anti-gun Initiative 676 in 1997; a measure that was backed by the state's then-Gov. Gary Locke, a Seattle Democrat, and other high-ranking Washington State Democrats.

Relatively speaking, gun owners do not often exert their political clout en masse, instead preferring gun rights organizations including the NRA, CCRKBA and GOA to do their talking, and not always do these groups get along with one another.

And that serves Hillary Diane Rodham Clinton very well, as does it also work for her allies in the gun control lobby, and her anti-gun Democrat colleagues in Congress. It allows Democrats to insist they support the gun rights of their constituents, while at the same time insisting that steps must be taken to tighten down on "the easy access to guns."

On the campaign trail, Hillary modified her rhetoric to say she is only against "illegal guns." The immediate question is what constitutes an "illegal gun" and who makes that determination?

According to reporter Jake Tapper's February 5, 2008 blog on ABC News' "Political Punch" website, she advocates a registry for "felons, people who have been committed to mental institutions like the man in Virginia Tech who caused so much death and havoc." It is surprising to many gun control advocates that resistance to such an idea has not come from the firearms community, but from the mental health community and its professionals who zealously guard the rights of mental patients.

Hillary has stated that she wants to take guns "out of the hands of young people." How does she propose to accomplish this? Will it mean, gun owners ask, that they can no longer teach their children to shoot and handle firearms responsibly? Does it mean that youths can no longer attend hunter education courses and subsequently go hunting with their parents and relatives? What is to happen to 4-H shooting programs for youths, not to mention the well-established Boy Scout marksmanship program?

Preposterous to ask such questions, you say? Hillary Clinton has supported "zero tolerance" laws and rules that have turned high school and even junior high and elementary students into criminals, or cost them suspensions or expulsions for such things as wearing T-shirts depicting firearms or the shooting sports, or drawing pictures of guns. She is a darling of the ultra-Left National Education Association, which has allowed "zero tolerance" enforcement to become a substitute for common sense.

It's the criminal, stupid

In the mid-1990s, well into Bill Clinton's reign as president, NRA Executive Vice President Wayne LaPierre went after the anti-gun president by paraphrasing something Clinton had said during his first campaign in 1992: "It's the economy, stupid."

In explaining where the problem with violent crime lay, LaPierre told the Clinton Administration, "It's the criminal, stupid!"

If the message was lost on the Clinton co-presidency, it resonated with the American people. By some estimates, there are 80 to 90 million gun owners in the United States and by the middle of Bill Clinton's second term, they were furious. They had been demonized for the mere fact that they owned firearms and wanted to exercise a constitutional right, they had been blamed for crimes they had not committed and had been deliberately relegated to the level of second-class citizens by a president and his administration, including the First Lady.

A decade has passed since LaPierre fired that shot across the Clinton bow, and in that time the semi-auto ban has expired and there is ample proof it never accomplished anything other than to inconvenience hundreds of thousands of law-abiding citizens and drive the prices of such firearms upwards for a ten-year period. But as noted earlier, the anti-gun movement is rather big on symbolism, and they seem more interested in putting that feather back in their cap than they are about taking steps that actually reduce crime and take criminals off the streets.

While Hillary Clinton occasionally falls back on her mantra of the late 1990s by observing, "We just have to figure out how we are going to get smart about protecting our kids," and Barack Obama says, "We need to do a more effective job of enforcing our gun laws," neither has put much emphasis on just how they are going to accomplish that.

Such vague statements are almost certainly designed to give gun owners the appearance that the candidates making them have no intention of further eroding the rights of gun owners, but as previous chapters have demonstrated, that is hardly the case.

The reason is simple, yet to date, nobody seems willing to address the basic fact that neither Hillary Clinton nor Barack Obama really had a solution that cracks down on criminals, while leaving honest gun owners alone.

95

Hillary wanted to register handguns. Barack wanted to ban them altogether. Then Hillary wanted to renew the ban on so-called "assault weapons," and so did Barack. Hillary wants a "gun summit." Barack wants to protect the rights of hunters and recreational shooters. Both now acknowledge that handgun bans aren't going to happen, and they know it is political suicide on a national scale to bring up such a proposal.

Well into the 2008 presidential primary season, neither candidate had said much if anything about the public's right to self-defense, about three-strikes laws that put violent offenders in prison for life with no possibility for parole after being convicted of a third felony.

Instead of talking about gun rights for hunters and regulatory measures that only affect law-abiding citizens, where was the talk, where *is* the talk, about adding prison space, about stopping illegal alien criminals, about putting an end to so-called "gun free zones?" What about a discussion on national concealed carry rights and state reciprocity requirements that would require each state to honor a concealed handgun license or permit issued by another state?

Why did Hillary Clinton not channel her husband's recognized gift of gab in the direction of fixing the criminal justice system, instead of allowing him to launch attacks on Sen. Obama that questioned his patriotism and qualifications? Why didn't she, why *won't* she, go after judges who are too liberal, lenient and lazy to throw the proverbial book at recidivist offenders who bounce from one crime to the next, and from one jurisdiction to another? Where has Sen. Clinton been while college students and professors are being systematically disarmed by hysteria that insists in a shrill collective voice that college campuses are safe when Virginia Tech and Northern Illinois University prove they are not?

While she spoke in platitudes and danced around the issue with such remarks as this, reported by the *Boston Globe* on February 19, 2008, "Violence of any kind should not be tolerated and hits too close to home when it's directed at our young people. America has witnessed school violence before and it is always tragic," she has said *nothing*.

The answer is simple. She had nothing to say critically about liberal judges because they are exactly the kind of judges she would have nominated to the federal bench, including the United States Supreme Court.

She has nothing to say about laws and campus rules that disarm instructors and students who could otherwise legally carry firearms for personal protection, when she spent so much effort championing the "gun free zone" philosophy.

And she is far less interested in keeping felons behind prison walls then she is about letting them vote. As far back as 2005, Hillary Clinton was advocating legislation that would allow convicted felons to regain their voting (but, of course, not their gun) rights.

In a March 7, 2005 essay that appeared in the *Wall Street Journal* under the headline "My Felon Americans," writer John Fund noted, "Mrs. Clinton says she is pushing her bill because she is opposed to 'disenfranchisement of legitimate American voters.' But it's hard not to suspect partisan motives. In a 2003 study, sociologists Chistopher Uggen and Jeff Manza found that roughly 4.2 million had been disfranchised nationwide, a third of whom had completed their prison time or parole. Taking into account the lower voter turnout of felons, they concluded that about one-third of them would vote in presidential races, and that would have overwhelmingly supported Democratic candidates."

Hillary has nothing against criminals, so long as they vote for her.

What is 'Reasonable?'

Throughout the history of gun control, right up to the Supreme Court challenge of the District of Columbia handgun ban, proponents of gun control have invariably couched their argument in terms of "reasonable regulation."

And that's how it has been for Hillary Diane Rodham Clinton, who would have us believe it is fine for convicted felons to vote (because they presumably vote overwhelmingly Democrat) but it is not so fine for law-abiding citizens to have firearms to protect themselves from the same felons.

("Oh, my God, they're shooting my constituents!")

Hillary is not alone. Barack Obama says, "I think there is an individual right to bear arms, but it's subject to common-sense regulation."

Check with any number of ranking Democrats in Congress and even in state legislatures and you will get a variation on this theme; "support" for the Second Amendment right "to own guns for hunting and target shooting" but that ownership should be subject to "reasonable regulation," those "common-sense gun safety" measures that gun control lobbyists constantly talk about.

One naturally is inclined to inquire about the definition of "common-sense regulation," but one will have to wait for the answer.

Hillary tells Chris Matthews during the Nevada debate: "You know, I believe in the Second Amendment. People have a right to bear arms but I also believe that we can common-sensically (sic) approach this."

The nation waits for her definition of "common-sensical," and we presume hopefully that it is something more than the definition of "is."

Therein lies the problem. One person's reasonable regulation is another person's constitutional outrage. Even Chief Justice John Roberts, during oral arguments in the case of *District of Columbia v Heller*, the celebrated Second Amendment challenge to the District's 32-year-old handgun ban, was compelled to ask "What is reasonable about (a ban)?"

Hillary thinks the gun laws of New York City are "reasonable" but a citizen in Buffalo, Wyoming might think far differently, and that citizen will vote for the person he or she wants to become president, and that will not be someone who supports restrictive gun laws.

This is not a problem of semantics but of social philosophy. It cannot have regional barriers, for a civil right that is exercised by a citizen in New York City should be the same civil right exercised by a citizen in Salt Lake City, and what is common sense in one venue is common sense in all venues.

Speaking in nebulous terms on the gun issue, or not speaking at all, is an issue with gun control proponents as well as gun rights activists. Even the traditionally anti-gun *Boston Globe* hinted at its frustration with Clinton and Obama when it headlined the February 19, 2008 article "Missing on gun control," as if to suggest that both candidates were "missing in action" on the gun issue. And during the presidential campaign, they essentially were.

Paul Helmke, president of the anti-gun Brady Campaign to Prevent Gun Violence, suggested to a *Boston Globe* reporter that there was no leadership by either Hillary Clinton or Barack Obama on the gun issue.

"I think a lot of candidates and politicians are afraid of getting the gun lobby upset," Helmke was quoted as stating. "They fear that talking about guns, it's gonna lose them elections."

It became apparent that if there was one thing on which Hillary Clinton and Barack Obama seemed to agree, it was that they would avoid the issue of gun control versus gun rights like the proverbial plague. Other than the lip service we have discussed earlier about "supporting the Second Amendment," neither candidate has been specific. Then, again, neither had to be since each had a track record, from which they deftly tried to back away.

And that is the essence of a gun control proponent who is also a politician. They establish a track record, then come election time when their votes come back to haunt them, they speak in generalities and become increasingly vague about where they stand, and where they stood. They "no longer hold that view" or acknowledge that they must be politically realistic...to the point of their re-election and then they can comfortably fall back on their core beliefs because by then the public is stuck with them for another term.

To push gun control, one must lull the public toward slumber, because a wide awake electorate has, time and again, demonstrated that it will not submit to the conscious erosion of that which they hold so dear: a fundamental individual civil right. In Massachusetts, California, Washington state and elsewhere, when a question about gun bans has been put to a public vote, the public rejects that proposition overwhelmingly.

Americans know, from watching the histories of other nations, and observing what disarmament has meant in places like Washington, D.C., Chicago, New York and Newark, to say nothing of Northern Illinois University, Trolley Square, Westroads Mall and Virginia Tech.

Hillary Diane Rodham Clinton wanted to be president, commander-in-chief, the first woman elected to the Oval Office. She insisted she is ready to lead.

Barack Obama wants to be president, commander-in-chief, the first African-American elected to the Oval Office. He insists he is ready to lead.

Together, they represent what may be wrong with the Democrats as a party. They want to *be* something when it is not entirely clear they want to *do* something, except, perhaps, when it comes to regulating firearms. At least, that is the way a huge segment of the American public sees Democrats, and that segment consists entirely of gun owners who have concluded that they do not need to be encumbered by any further "common sense regulation" of their firearms.

Americans want a leader who trusts the citizens to be as responsible with their firearms as they are with their vote. They are looking for a leader who will express outrage over a civil rights atrocity like the New Orleans gun confiscation and prevent that from ever happening again. They want a leader who does not merely "support the Second Amendment" but lives it. They desire a leader who is more interested in doing something than in simply being something.

Hillary Clinton has ambition. She wants authority. Barack Obama has ambition, and he also wants authority.

Both insist they have experience and want America to trust them, but based on their track records, and the record of the party they represent, American gun owners aren't having any of it.

Their actions have spoken louder than words, and their records tell the firearms community all they need to know.

One might sum it up by observing that when the future of America, and particularly the integrity of a fundamental civil right is at stake, everybody "has a dog in that fight."

And when one puts it in that perspective, then takes an accounting of what Hillary Clinton, Barack Obama and other Democrats have done, and might do, one must conclude "these dogs don't hunt."

Ten

THE 'CLINTON LEGACY'

Every president of the United States wants to establish a legacy; some mark to show not only that he was in office, but more importantly that he accomplished some great thing that has a lasting impact on the nation.

William Jefferson Clinton's legacy is currently dubious in nature; a presidency that became a national embarrassment, complete with a standard of lying and denial that it provides something of a benchmark against which other scandals, such as Eliot Spitzer's fall from grace as governor of New York in early 2008, are now invariably measured.

Perspective has much to do with how someone's legacy is perceived. Steadfast Clinton admirers – those willing to overlook the former president's penchant for "spinning the facts" – will cite many reasons that he will be remembered as a great president. They will cite the relative prosperity (forgetting, naturally, that much of this was due to Republican budgets) and the relative domestic tranquility, which took a sharp and irreversible turn on the morning of September 11, 2001, barely eight months into the George W. Bush presidency.

Clinton detractors have a far different perspective. He will be remembered as the president who failed to act on Osama bin Laden when he had the opportunity. He's the man who spent too much time trying to disarm law-abiding citizens and too little time working to lock up criminals. His attorney general presided over the botched operation that burned the Branch Davidian compound outside of Waco to the ground and she also sent Elian Gonzales back to Communist Cuba. Bill Clinton's policies, they would argue, have crippled America from becoming energy independent. He left more marks on the office than merely a semen stain on a blue dress, they will insist.

So, years after Bill Clinton left office, what is his legacy?

Hillary Diane Rodham Clinton, her service in the Senate and her campaign for the White House. That was a big part of his legacy.

The former First Lady who stuck by him – for whatever reasons – would have become Bill Clinton's new claim to fame should she have risen to the office of president of the United States, and made history as the first woman to occupy that office.

Where he failed as a president, he would possibly have succeeded by making her president, and then she could theoretically take up where he left off, pushing through socialized medicine, establishing a record upon which he can somehow figure a way to rest his narcissistic laurels, and bring him back more into the popular limelight, if only by default. Oh, and Hillary would presumably push the gun control initiatives Bill wanted, but could not quite squeak through Congress prior to November 1994, and never had a prayer of pushing after that.

Of course, all of this was predicated upon Hillary Clinton getting her party's nomination and then winning the election.

That's no small task for a politician who is still reasonably well-liked, but as Spring 2008 unfolded, it became obvious to all but the most loyal and perhaps legally blind Bill and Hillary Clinton supporters that Hillary's veneer of likeability had worn pretty thin. Where the press appeared to be enamored with Hillary one year before, they had now become far more scrutinizing and critical, especially since they now had someone else over whom to dote: Barack Obama. It appears Democrats may be glad to be rid of the Clintons.

Writing in the *New York Daily News* on March 31, 2008, columnist Stanley Crouch observed, "On TV, Clinton seems by turns icy, contrived, hysterical, sentimental, bitter, manipulative and self-righteous. In short, dehumanized by the mysterious dictates of technology, she takes on qualities that most people hate."

Perhaps not to be outdone, Christopher Hitchens wrote in *Slate* on the same day, as he discussed Hillary's embarrassing stumble over the Bosnia story that fell apart on national television, "...Sen. Clinton, given repeated chances to modify her absurd claim to have operated under fire while in the company of her then-16-year-old daughter and a USO entertainment troupe, kept up a stone-faced and self-loving insistence that, yes, she had exposed herself to sniper fire in the cause of gaining moral credit and, perhaps to be banked for the future, national-security "experience." This must mean either a) that she lies without conscience or reflection; or b) that she is subject to fantasies of an illusory past; or c) both of the above. Any of the foregoing would constitute a disqualification for the presidency of the United States."

All of this adversity only brought Bill Clinton into the fight more strenuously, for he was not simply defending his loyal spouse, he was defending his living legacy; his last, best hope to perhaps square his image with the nation beyond the confines of his own faithful by getting his wife elected president. As the San Jose Mercury News noted, also on March 31, 2008 – when a growing list of powerful Democrats were urging and encouraging Hillary to drop out of the race to avoid a political donnybrook at the national convention – Bill Clinton was demanding that people "chill out."

It is both ironic and telling that, according to the *San Francisco Chronicle* of April 2, 2008, in the moments leading up to Bill Clinton's remarks to a group of super-delegates in California, the former president himself had a rather heated moment with a delegate identified as Rachel Binah, formerly a supporter of Bill Richardson who had switched to supporting Hillary.

The newspaper account said Binah approached Bill Clinton and observed how "sorry" she was that Clinton attack dog James Carville had called Bill Richardson a "Judas" for having endorsed Barack Obama. It was then, the news account said, that Clinton lost it, raging that Richardson had told him "Five times to my face...that he would never do that."

Clinton then launched into an attack on the media for its "unfair treatment" of his candidate wife, apparently because reporters were no longer tossing her softball questions, but serious queries about her qualifications and her untruthful accounts about events in Bosnia and how she had spoken to daughter, Chelsea, on the morning of September 11, 2001.

As only Bill Clinton could do, he then put on a happy face, stepped out onto the stage and put a spin on his wife's downward spiraling standing against Barack Obama that had her winning the nomination and in the process, making the party stronger, not weaker.

"We are going to win this election if we just chill out and let everybody have their say," Clinton stated, according to the newspaper account.

Perhaps he was anticipating a similar victory for Hillary to one he eked out in 1992 only due to the intervention of populist spoiler candidate H. Ross Perot. Remember that Perot had bailed out of the presidential campaign in July of that year when his name was on the ballot in only about half of the states. He charged right back in again in October after his name was put on the ballots in all 50 states, and when it appeared Clinton was losing ground to Perot's real arch-foe, George H.W. Bush, the man whom Perot was determined to bring down, with his own strength or by helping Clinton win the presidency.

There would be no H. Ross Perot in 2008, and Hillary Clinton was on her own, and putting up as good a fight as one might expect from a person who had imagined herself easily strolling to the nomination, before she was hit by the Obama tidal wave.

But Obama was finding no easy road to the nomination, either, with Hillary determined to stay in the fight even when it became clear, according to network pundits and "political analysts" that the delegate math simply was not with her, even after her second resurrection in Pennsylvania. If 2008 demonstrated anything, it was that Democrats have some noisy skeletons in their closets. For Hillary, it seemed to be one gaffe or stumble after another, and for Barack Obama, it was the "God Damn America" rantings of his pastor and mentor, the Rev. Jeremiah Wright, and his own lack of depth and experience.

More than one observer has noted that Obama is a "marvelous speaker" but he says nothing of substance, and an hour after hearing an Obama speech, one may be hungry for more, but will be left essentially with an unsatisfied appetite.

Meanwhile, Hillary garnered support from the faithful feminists, who continued encouraging her to stay in the race and subsequently threatened to vote for John McCain. As the Associated Press and *Seattle Post-Intelligencer* reported, also coincidentally on March 31, 2008, "Amid mounting calls from top Democrats for Clinton to step aside and clear the path for rival Barack Obama, strategists are warning of damage to the party's chances in November if women – who make up the majority of Democratic voters nationwide, but especially the older, white working-class women who've long formed the former first lady's base – sense that a mostly male party establishment is unfairly muscling Clinton out of the race."

At this point, one might easily suggest that the "party of diversity" had been showing its rather questionable soul; on the one hand it encourages liberal women, but on the other hand wants their leader to stand down. Of course, by the same token (no pun intended), were the shoe on the other foot, the party might be challenged for insulting its black constituents if many of its more prominent leaders had urged Obama to step aside for Hillary. It's something of a "lose-lose" situation.

Hillary's 'Last Stand?'

How does one judge their own career? How does history judge a person's life? Does it look hard at accomplishments or failures; does it base the judgment on a single act?

People remember George Armstrong Custer not for his remarkable achievements during the Civil War, but for the final 45 minutes of his life, which became one of the nation's worst military disasters, an entire command wiped out thanks to a colossally foolish tactical error. Yet more than 130 years later, Custer still stands as something of a hero, but the fact remains that he got himself killed in the process, along with the men who followed him down the east slopes of the Little Bighorn Valley.

Vowing to fight to the bitter end is judged by some to be the mark of courage. After all, the defenders of the Alamo have been lionized for their heroism in fighting to the bitter end, even when they knew they were doomed.

In presidential politics, however, fighting to the bitter end often means ultimate humiliation – something people who aspire to be president cannot accept graciously or otherwise –and it occasionally means they leave their party in a shambles. They're not wiped out like the troopers of the 7th Cavalry, but a lot of political blood gets spilled.

For narcissistic egomaniacs, that is often preferable to being the "good loser." Many would rather go down in flames and take everyone else with them rather than face the acknowledgement that they were not the "people's choice."

To be a good loser, one also must be a "good winner," and there is no history of that behavior in Hillary Clinton's past. But going into the Democratic campaign for president, Hillary never had the slightest notion that she might lose her party's nomination, especially to some upstart less-than-one-term freshman senator from Illinois. This was to have been a coronation cake walk. A free ride from the press.

Good losers do not turn loose the likes of James Carville on anyone, be they a nobody like Paula Jones or a highly-respected career public servant and politician like New Mexico's Bill Richardson. But Carville has always been an attack dog for the Clintons, and at times it appears he has no other talent. Lucky for him he was not actually born a canine, else he would long ago have been neutered, if not euthanized.

Some might presume that the appearance of Carville in the primary fray was a signal that a very desperate Hillary had pulled out all the stops. After all, she was lagging behind Obama in delegates and popularity across much of the political landscape, and historically, when the Clinton gloves have come off, it has been Carville's knuckles that landed the punches.

Leading up to the Pennsylvania primary, it was clear that Hillary was forgetting herself in ways that even Bill Clinton and James Carville could be of no help, because she pretty much cut any ties that may have existed with gun owners when she told the *Pittsburgh Tribune-Review* that "we should reinstate the assault weapons ban," despite strong evidence that the ten-year ban, signed into law by her husband in 1994 – leading to the devastating congressional defeat for Democrats in November of that year – had no significant impact on crime.

But there was a possibility that Hillary did not believe she would need any help, at least where gun-owning Keystone State Democrats were concerned. When Barack Obama, three weeks before the primary vote, did what some observers would consider an act of political suicide by telling the *Pittsburgh Tribune-Review* on April 1 that he did not support the idea of private citizens carrying concealed handguns for their own protection, he handed Hillary the first of two opportunities to actually appear to be the better candidate on the gun issue (the other being his horribly insensitive comment about clinging to guns and religion).

"I am not in favor of concealed weapons," Obama told the newspaper. "I think that creates a potential atmosphere where more innocent people could (get shot during) altercations."

Reaction to that remark was swift and blistering. The Citizens Committee for the Right to Keep and Bear Arms demanded that Obama issue an apology, and accused the senator of "confusing legally-armed, law-abiding Americans with inner-city thugs, gang-bangers and other criminals who carry guns illegally."

"Barack Obama ignorantly believes that legally-armed Americans are as reckless and irresponsible as the criminals with whom his political sympathies evidently lay," CCRKBA said. "He has been insisting for months that he supports the Second Amendment right to keep and bear arms, but here he is now campaigning in Pennsylvania, stating essentially that he would prefer Americans not exercise that right."

The *Tribune-Review*, in an April 2 report, somewhat coyly noted that the gun control positions of Clinton, Obama and Republican nominee Sen. John McCain "may figure in" the Pennsylvania vote. That was certainly an understatement, with more than a million gun owners in a state with the largest number of NRA members of any state in the union.

One week after Hillary and Obama made their anti-gun remarks, Pennsylvania gun owners held the third annual Gun Rights Rally at the capitol in Harrisburg. That gathering left no uncertainties where many Pennsylvanians stood on the gun rights issue.

But does it matter to Hillary Clinton, junior senator from New York State?

Would it have mattered to Hillary Clinton, president of the United States?

Likewise, would it matter to Barack Obama, junior senator from Illinois, or the same Barack Obama if he were to become president?

Alas, things like that matter only when one is *running* for office, not after someone has taken the oath of office.

There has been, and will remain, a legitimate concern among America's gun owners that a return of a Democrat to the White House, supported by strong Democrat majorities in both houses of Congress, would foster in a new Dark Age for gun ownership, despite anything the Supreme Court might say about the right to keep and bear arms.

During the first two years of the Bill Clinton administration, perennial anti-gunners on Capitol Hill, including then-Congressman Charles Schumer, arrogantly told gun owners that their "worst nightmare had come true." Their arrogance turned to angst in November 2004 when they learned that pushing through the Brady Law and the Clinton ban on sport-utility rifles and full-capacity ammunition magazines brought down the wrath of gun owners on Democrats across the nation. Even then-House Speaker Thomas Foley of Washington State was not spared.

Whether that lesson has been lost on Democrats as a party one can only speculate. It appears to have been lost on many Democrat leaders in Congress, and most assuredly on those who would run for president.

When a political party loses sight of its responsibilities to a nation and *all* of its citizens, including those who choose to exercise their gun rights and own firearms, it surrenders whatever right it might perceive to provide leadership.

When a politician loses perspective that they are elected to *serve*, rather than *reign*, that individual surrenders his or her soul. For it is not the privilege to lead but the power to control that such people seek.

Look at Hillary Clinton's record as a United States Senator and one sees scant evidence that she has accomplished much of anything. She has attached her name to some legislation, and sponsored a couple of minor measures, but this woman who would be president had really done no significant thing or built a tangible foundation upon which to justifiably base her claims that she has the experience and qualifications to lead the nation.

Were she to publicly declare that she had been integral to the decision-making process of her husband's administration might harm more than help her campaign, particularly among voting blocs upon which she would depend in a match up against Republican John McCain, or anyone else with his stature. It would remind the American public that this woman was never elected in 1992, her husband was, and despite the suggestion by Bill Clinton that voters would be "getting two for the price of one," that notion has never really set well with the majority of Americans.

In the final analysis, one must accept that the Clinton "aura" has been built on foundation of lies, and that both Hillary and Bill habitually do it, and frequently get caught at it. For Bill, it was a stained blue dress. For Hillary, it was a landing in Bosnia under sniper fire and a tale about daughter Chelsea's whereabouts on 9/11.

So, while the political legacy of William Jefferson Clinton might well be hinged on how his wife is remembered, and while Hillary Diane Rodham Clinton's political legacy is perhaps yet to be written, their historical legacy could easily be a combination of damage they did to the Democratic Party and the lies they told in the process. It may take years for the party to heal.

Bill Clinton's efforts to damage gun rights in the United States cost Democrats control of Congress for 12 years. Had Hillary Clinton won the nomination and gone on as president, and certainly the election of Barack Obama as president could easily cost Democrats control of Congress forever.

Eleven

THE GANG CAN'T SHOOT STRAIGHT

Being a "straight shooter" in the traditional term is being trustworthy, to say what you mean and back it up, and to tell things the way you see them to be, regardless whether it may be politically correct.

Alas, on the subject of gun control and gun rights, Democrats as a party have not been straight shooters for decades, their rhetoric to the contrary. Indeed, it is because of the chasm between what they say and how they vote that they have been anointed as not-so-straight-shooters.

Perhaps their greatest sin is arrogance. Democrats engineered and bitterly defended the gun ban in the District of Columbia, and the issue ended up before the Supreme Court of the United States when all the city would have had to do to moot the case was change a few words in their ordinance and allow rifles and shotguns to be kept in working order for home defense. They fought the case because they thought they would prevail, because they foolishly believed that their will would win out over the rule of law.

A Democrat administration in New Orleans initiated the post-Katrina gun seizure and then steadfastly fought a federal court order stopping it, all the while denying the ban took place until the evidence was revealed in a couple of cargo containers.

Democrats ignored warnings and history in San Francisco by putting a handgun ban on the ballot and then defending the measure which they clearly knew was illegal, all the way to the State Supreme Court. Not once, but twice!

They are not defending what they necessarily believe is right, they are defending their self-ordained authority to dictate the human condition, whether it involves public behavior or personal values and beliefs. They have embraced the notion that they are wiser than the people (the same "people" identified in the First, Second, Fourth, Ninth and Tenth amendments).

In essence, too many Democrats have become "Nanny Statists," that is, they believe that they are protectors of the public at large rather than servants of the people who elected them to office. In the process of evolving to this level, which has gone beyond the realm of mere stereotype, they have concluded that they can tell the public anything, no matter how outrageously their words are belied by their deeds, and get away with it.

Barack Obama and Hillary Clinton, for example, have taken positions that they "support the Second Amendment as an individual right," while at the same time arguing that this right can and should be subject to all manner of regulations. The same holds true for many other Democrats who have "talked the talk" but have failed miserably in "walking the walk."

A "right" that is regulated to the point of irrelevancy is not a right at all, but a privilege that can be given and taken away with nothing more than a voice vote (so no votes are recorded) and the stroke of an executive's pen. This is a concept that Democrats such as Charles Schumer and Harry Reid do not seem to grasp, or have grasped all-too-well, while gun rights advocates long ago realized the consequences and talked about them openly, only to be ignored as though they were ignorant conspiracy theorists.

Some years ago, when Dr. Suzanna Gratia Hupp, a Texas resident who later rose to become a state legislator and champion of that state's concealed carry statute, testified before Congress, she made a statement that alarmed members of the House Judiciary panel to whom she was speaking. There is no small amount of irony in the fact that, at the time, Charles Schumer was still in the House of Representatives and he was sitting on that panel.

Dr. Hupp's parents were victims of the Luby's Cafeteria massacre perpetrated by madman George Hennard on October 16, 1991. Hupp was there when it happened and saw both of her parents murdered. As she spoke in support of gun rights and protecting the Second Amendment, she reminded the panel that this civil right is not merely in the Bill of Rights so that people can go hunting or target shooting.

Staring intently at the panel and speaking in a measured tone, she told House members that the Second Amendment is "about all of our rights to be able to protect ourselves from all of you guys up there."

This comes down to a matter of trust, and American gun owners have long since decided that they cannot trust Democrats, as a party and in most cases as individuals, because the individuals will eventually succumb to party pressure.

So, when you have Barack Obama saying, "I am not in favor of concealed weapons. I think that creates a potential atmosphere where more innocent people could (get shot during) altercations," it tells American gun owners that his rhetoric about supporting the Second Amendment is lip service.

When a nasty zealot like Charles Schumer can boast that "We're here to tell the NRA their nightmare is true! We're going to hammer guns on ... We're going to beat guns into submission," you have the real Democrat coming out from behind the slick, packaged message. This is the genuine article, unbridled by the need to curry voter favor because he is in the majority party and he knows that anything his colleagues do will be hard to undo.

When Obama tells a crowd during a fundraiser in upscale San Francisco that, "You go into some of these small towns in Pennsylvania, and like a lot of small towns in the Midwest, the jobs have been gone now for 25 years and nothing's replaced them. And they fell through the Clinton administration, and the Bush administration, and each successive administration has said that somehow these communities are gonna regenerate and they have not. So it's not surprising then that they get bitter, they cling to guns or religion or antipathy to people who aren't like them or anti-immigrant sentiment or anti-trade sentiment as a way to explain their frustrations," you get the impression he is speaking as an elitist member of an exclusive club that takes minorities and women for granted and looks upon conservatives as ignorant rubes.

Why else, one could ask, have Far Left Democrats declared themselves "progressives?" Probably because nobody else would, considering that their programs have hardly reflected any semblance of progress. Strictly on the issue of guns, their gun control agenda has resulted in the creation of "Zero Tolerance" policies that substitute inflexibility for common sense. Their policies have invented "Gun Free Zones," where all too many times some demented killer has found a target rich environment and no resistance from his victims because they have been disarmed by regulations.

All of this has come about, say critics within the gun community, because of a rising arrogance that has permeated the party, creating an attitude among its Left-leaning members and leaders that they are better able to make decisions for all the people than the people, themselves.

It was perhaps best described in a comment from a reader of the *Seattle Post-Intelligencer* as a "sneering arrogance and smug self-righteousness."

This is the reality versus the masquerade. Schumer and Reid, as noted in Chapter Two, went out and recruited a pro-gun Democrat to run for the U.S. Senate in Ohio, only to subsequently, and rather unceremoniously, dump the man in favor of a Congressional insider who also happens to be consistently anti-gun.

Dianne Feinstein admits to a *60 Minutes* crew that she would have banned and confiscated semi-auto rifles if she had only been able to get a few more votes in the Senate.

Political writers note repeatedly that the Democrats started changing their rhetoric and re-packaging their message in order to win back Congress, but they say nothing about the party actually changing its philosophy on gun rights. At this point, it would require a repudiation of decades of political posturing, and the party will not do it.

Hillary Clinton bashes Barack Obama for his condescending attitude toward rural Pennsylvanians while mentioning that she learned to shoot as a youngster, but then brushes off questions from reporters wanting to know when was the last time she fired a gun.

This is where the proverbial rubber should meet the road, but in the case of the National Democratic Party and gun rights, there is a nail in the tire and it is quickly losing air.

Running versus Hiding

"You can run, but you can't hide."

That might be the most applicable adage for Democrat Party leaders and their effort to distance themselves from their own ideology. They would require political plastic surgery, because their votes are public record, their statements to the press are archived, their blustering threats made against gun owners, gun makers and gun rights organizations during the heyday of gun control in the 1980s and 1990s are available by simply searching the Internet.

It is impossible to hide the past, or hide from it, when the past is littered with headlines like this from Newsmax.com from February 25, 2004: "Senate Democrats Push Anti-gun Measures." That story noted, "Renewing the 1994 prohibition against 'assault weapons' has been a Democrat priority this year."

One cannot erase story leads like the one appearing in the December 17, 2005 edition of the *Boston Globe* under reporter Susan Milligan's byline that stated, "The Democratic Party, long identified with gun control, is rethinking its approach to the gun debate, seeking to improve the chances of its candidates in Western states where hunters have been wary of casting votes for a party with a national reputation of being against guns."

The problem gets even more challenging when Left Liberal special interest groups that traditionally support the Democratic Party (and arguably push it farther to the left) make the kinds of observations that were offered in early 2007 by the Santa Barbara Coalition Against Gun Violence, in a diatribe against legislation that prevents legal fishing expeditions to be conducted by providing access to sensitive gun trace data gathered by the federal Bureau of Alcohol, Tobacco, Firearms and Explosives.

"With Congress now under control of the Democrats," the group's newsletter opined, "who are generally more favorable to gun control..." the legislation might be rescinded.

Democrats cannot run much less hide from their history when their own support groups candidly identify the party as "more favorable to gun control."

It gets worse for Democrats when one accesses information on how much money they received from gun control groups during election cycles over the past several years. According to the website OpenSecrets.org, the "gun control industry" overwhelmingly sends money to Democrats, and relative table scraps to Republicans. In 2000, for example, donations to Democrats totaled $492,599, while Republicans reportedly got a paltry $13,000.

In 2002, contributions from gun control groups and individual gun control supporters came to $137,125. By 2004, the figure had started dwindling to $93,700 and in 2006, according to the website's figures, gun control groups and individuals donated $44,596 to Democrats.

On the other hand, Republicans were beneficiaries of overwhelming support from gun owners and gun rights organizations, which sees that party as much friendlier to firearms rights. So, one might conclude that the financial support issue sort of balances itself out.

But returning to the issue of Democrats being unable to hide from their past positions on gun control, they keep putting their feet in their mouths with gun owners when they have the kinds of exchanges that Hillary and Obama had with ABC's Charles Gibson and George Stephanopoulos during the April 2008 debate in Pennsylvania.

According to the transcript of that exchange, provided by the Federal News Service and available on the *New York Times* website, both Barack Obama and Hillary Clinton reflexively fell back on their gun control philosophies while professing to support an individual right to keep and bear arms.

Explaining his position on the Supreme Court's consideration of the lawsuit seeking to overturn the District of Columbia's handgun ban, Senator Obama was not able to successfully dance around his true attitudes.

"As a general principle," Obama stated, "I believe that the Constitution confers an individual right to bear arms. But just because you have an individual right does not mean that the state or local government can't constrain the exercise of that right, and, you know, in the same way that we have a right to private property but local governments can establish zoning ordinances that determine how you can use it."

Critics in the firearms community were quick to dismiss this as a specious position that would never be applied by Obama to the First Amendment right of free speech or freedom of the press. They also argued that Obama, without flatly stating it, essentially admitted that he supported the District's gun ban by endorsing the notion of local government control of firearms within their jurisdictions.

Obama subsequently lied about the fact that his handwriting appeared on a questionnaire filled out in 1996 when he was running for Illinois State Senate that clearly said he supported a ban on handguns.

No," he told Gibson, "my writing wasn't on that particular questionnaire, Charlie. As I said, I have never favored an all-out ban on handguns.

What I think we can provide," he continued, falling back on the rhetoric of the gun-ban lobby, "is common-sense approaches to the issue of illegal guns that are ending up on the streets. We can make sure that criminals don't have guns in their hands. We can make certain that those who are mentally deranged are not getting a hold of handguns."

Hillary did not do much better. She told Gibson, "What I favor is what works in New York," subsequently admitting, "What might work in New York City is certainly not going to work in Montana. So, for the federal government to be having any kind of, you know, blanket rules that they're going to try to impose, I think doesn't make sense."

Before a chorus breaks out into "Halleluiah," keep in mind that the gun control movement has been one of shifting sands and fixed goals. For a time, gun control activists found favor for "one-size-fits-all" national gun laws on Capitol Hill, but after gun owners took Congress away from Democrats and handed it to the Republicans in 1994, thus bringing a significant change in attitude about nationwide gun measures, the gun control lobby got busy in state legislatures, arguing ironically that local laws should be established to address local situations.

The objective has not changed at all: Gun control at all levels, the more the better.

Democrats are elitists

From none other than Left liberal icon Whoopi Goldberg came this startling admission in April 2008: "Well, what's the matter is that Democrats are an elitist group. That's the truth."

This remark was made on the Women on the Web forum, and if Goldberg thinks that, it must be true. It did not get much notice, except for a mention on Internet muckraker Matt Drudge's website.

But Democrats *are* elitist, and they have demonstrated this on many occasions, particularly as it applies to firearms. Dianne Feinstein, for example, had a concealed handgun permit, but has consistently backed gun control measures affecting her constituents and all other Americans. Ted Kennedy has had armed guards, including one who was arrested on Capitol Hill for carrying a weapon.

What Democrats have also demonstrated is their belief that gun owners are as gullible as other groups, which may explain why the Democrat Leadership Council has been so involved in the creation and support of the American Hunters and Shooters Association (AHSA) mentioned in Chapter Two. Headed by former NFL football player and one-time Democrat candidate for Maryland governor, Ray Schoenke, AHSA has billed itself as an alternative to the NRA, which has been blamed for the 1994 election taking Congress away from the party for the first time in 40 years.

Democrats love the AHSA because the organization gives them "cover" endorsements, providing the illusion that hunters and shooters support gun-grabbing career politicians. AHSA supports the efforts of the anti-gun Mayors Against Illegal Guns. In 2007, the AHSA held a press conference in St. Louis,

Missouri when the NRA was having its annual convention in that city. The press event was at a hotel about one block away from the convention center, and it was at that event that Schoenke and others from AHSA made it clear their intent is to pull members away from the NRA, thereby diluting the NRA's effectiveness even in some small way.

AHSA's endorsement of Barack Obama left no question in the minds of veteran gun rights activists that this organization is little more than a shill for Democrats regardless of their stand on gun ownership and the Second Amendment. But this would enable Obama to parade around states like Pennsylvania, Oregon and Washington claiming to have the support of sportsmen and gun owners.

AHSA is a creation of Gerry Kavanaugh, president of DCS Congressional and an advisor to John Edwards, the Democrat who can be seen on a YouTube video stating that he believes owning a handgun should be a privilege, not a right. What is DCS Congressional? According to its website, it is "a company that offers comprehensive Internet programs to Members of Congress, Democratic campaigns, advocacy organizations and state parties."

One of the founding members of DCS Congressional is former Democrat Congressman David Bonior, a perennial anti-gunner when he was in Congress. Another is former Democrat Congressman from New York, Thomas Downey.

As for Schoenke, he has contributed thousands of dollars to anti-gun Democrats over the past several years, including Bonior, Dianne Feinstein, John Kerry, Robert Torricelli, Bill Clinton, Barbara Boxer, Al Gore and Edward M. Kennedy.

To suggest that AHSA is non-partisan might be a stretch of credibility, much the same as the previously-mentioned Union Sportsman Alliance discussed in Chapter Five. The creation of AHSA does suggest, as noted earlier, that the principals behind it believe average sportsmen and women, and average gun owners might be easily enticed into its ranks and away from the NRA and other gun rights organizations, at least long enough to swell the AHSA ranks during an election cycle in order to convince the press and public that the sportsman/gun owner vote is split.

Quite possibly the best summation of Democrat elitism came from writer Mark Hemingway in a short essay appearing on the *National Review* Online website. He was discussing Obama's "god and guns" gaffe prior to the Pennsylvania primary, and how Obama and his fans in the media had tried to gloss it over. The portrait of Obama and how he responded to criticism of the remark might possibly reflect how far too many Democrats view their world.

"Whatever you want to make of Obama's diverse background prior to his adult forays into the Ivy League," Hemingway wrote, "liberal activism, and politics, his remarks seemed to suggest that it is this latter experience with those elitist institutions that define the world Obama inhabits. One where he's certain of what's best for people, and if only they weren't so distracted by this First and Second Amendment nonsense, they could hand him the reins of power tomorrow."

Yes, it is tough to control the flock when the sheep realize their shepherd is a wolf dressed in designer clothing.

Democrats and the Pogo Principle

Cartoonist Walt Kelly, creator of the popular "Pogo" comic strip, used the quote "We have met the enemy and he is us" on a poster for Earth Day, and the quote has become part of the American lexicon. It might well be called the "Pogo Principle." It might also explain why the Democratic Party, so long as it is under the control of Far Left anti-gun, would-be social engineers, will never enjoy the trust of America's 80-plus million gun owners.

Democrats are their own worst enemies because they define gun owners as the enemy, and have for years.

This is perhaps best exemplified by how former President Bill Clinton reacted to the defeat in 1994 of so many Democrats who voted for his ban on so-called "assault weapons." He told reporters, after blaming the NRA for the tidal wave election that took both houses of Congress away from the Democrats for the first time in 40 years, that the gun rights organization "had enough votes in New Hampshire, in Arkansas, maybe in Tennessee and Missouri to beat us and they whipped us in a few other places."

This was a defining statement: Democrats see a huge segment of America's population as "them" against "us." America's gun owners did not pick the fight which led to this collision of values, and it must have come as something of a surprise, if not downright shock, that gun owners did not obediently and passively roll over and accept what they saw as the destruction of a fundamental individual civil right, a cornerstone of the Bill of Rights. After all, even in the early days of the gun control movement, Democrats drifting further to the Left were beginning to see themselves as more capable of making serious decisions about the direction of the country, and about personal lifestyles, than the millions of other citizens, particularly citizens with firearms. This is the arrogance alluded to earlier in this chapter, an arrogance of elitism that permeates the party from its leadership to its neighborhood and college campus activists.

Witness what a Minnesota group, the Carleton Democrats based at Carleton College in Northfield – the town made famous when its armed citizens turned out en masse to shoot the Jesse James gang to pieces during a botched bank robbery in September 1876, just a few months after the Custer massacre at Little Bighorn in Montana – to get an assessment of what the next generation of Democrats believes:

"It is obvious that there are bigger problems in urban America. There are problems of poverty, violence, addiction, crime etc. These problems are intricately connected and if solved will take a national effort.

"Guns must still be removed...

"What we need are sensible gun regulations that make it as difficult as possible to obtain weapons with only occasional minor allowances where absolutely necessary...We must come together and face the issues of gun control. We must fight back against the NRA's red herrings (guns=freedom) and realize that regulating guns will cause it to be harder to purchase and use guns..."

They end this diatribe with the observation that "guns magnify all problems to a level that cannot be allowed in any society."

These are the student leaders who may someday guide the Democratic Party, the same party that championed gun control against millions of law-abiding citizens who had committed no crime, and suddenly found themselves being legislated against, as though they had. Some gun rights activists have suggested over the years that the reason the Far Left seems to have a phobia about firearms is that so long as guns remain in the hands of the people, the people will be quite able to make their own decisions about all of the things the Far Left Democrats believe only they are qualified to decide.

Simplistic? Perhaps, but then, again perhaps not.

Democrats had as a plank in their platform in 2000 language that would micro-manage the way a gun owner could first obtain and then legally keep and store a firearm. Their position was simple, and spelled out in their national platform dated August 15, 2000: "We need mandatory child safety locks. We should require a photo license I.D., a background check, and a gun safety test to buy a new handgun."

This came from people who have had little or no personal experience with firearms.

In his straightforward assessment of the 2008 Democratic presidential frontrunners that appeared in the April 17, 2008 edition of the *Wall Street Journal*, attorney David Kopel, research director for the Independence Institute, noted how silly it was to see Hillary Clinton and Barack Obama campaigning around Pennsylvania competing for the pro-gun vote. He compared it to "an election race of Pat Robertson versus James Dobson, each of them appearing at organic grocery stores and Starbucks throughout Massachusetts, with each candidate insisting that he alone deserves the vote of gay-marriage advocates."

Gun owners know that neither Clinton nor Obama are or ever will be seriously in their corner, yet they and other leading Democrats have, perhaps living in a self-induced state of denial, somehow convinced themselves that they must try to woo the "gun vote" because it was angry gun owners who changed Congress in 1994, deprived Al Gore of the White House in 2000 and prevented John Kerry from becoming president in 2004, and the Democrats know it.

After years of this "say one thing, do another" gamesmanship, the Democrat party remains a study in self-delusional behavior if not world class hypocrisy because its leaders insist on appealing to gun owners while continually voting against their interests.   They have been unable to sell their notion of "sensible gun laws" because gun owners do not consider them sensible at all, the same as they recognize that "gun safety" in the Democrat lexicon is merely a semantic substitute for "gun control."

In the final analysis, if Democrats ever hope to regain the trust of American gun owners that they carelessly dismissed and then arrogantly demonized a generation ago in their quest to establish some sort of moral Utopia, the party must renounce years of systematic erosion of a cherished civil right and repudiate the architects of that effort. It is not enough to claim fealty to gun owners and "support" for the Second Amendment, the party must once again "live" the Second Amendment as it lives up to, and defends, rights protected by all the other Amendments in the Bill of Rights.

For perennial gun haters Frank Lautenberg, Charles Schumer, Jesse Jackson, John Kerry, Al Gore, Dianne Feinstein, Edward Kennedy, Barack Obama, Bill and Hillary Clinton and scores of others in Congress and in the halls of state legislatures from Maine to Hawaii, that may simply not be possible.

They have left their mark on the Democratic Party, much like a stain that refuses to be washed out. It was they, and others like them, all with that "D" behind their name, that cried havoc and let slip the dogs of political war, not the tens of millions of hunters, gun collectors, competition shooters, armed citizens all who have been marginalized, ignored, and insulted, and who finally decided to fight back.

That the Democrats have been unable to grasp the concept of this political resistance only reinforces the belief that, as a party and as a cultural group, they have forgotten the roots of the Second Amendment and how this nation was created, first through political resistance and finally through force of arms. And failing to understand that this is really what the Second Amendment is all about means they can no longer enjoy the respect they may have once had from America's firearms community, and perhaps they never will.

Twelve

MEANWHILE, WAITING IN THE WINGS...

Emerging as the nominee and standard bearer for the Democrats in 2008, freshman Senator Barack Obama ran his campaign promising change. Everyone wants it, far too many people cannot define it, and when – and if – it actually occurs, it looks exactly like that which it was designed to replace.

Such "change" typically tends to disenfranchise those who do not blindly embrace it. In the case of a far-Left Liberal Democrat like Barack Obama, and a crop of "rising stars" along with perennial Democrat standard-bearers, disenfranchisement would immediately apply to anyone who owns a firearm, and especially those who own guns for personal protection and exercise their right to carry that firearm in public.

Obama is one man, who could not change the anti-gun sentiment of his party, even if he wanted to, which he does not. His remarks against concealed carry, and his voting record in Illinois, suggests that he does not want a reversal of his party's stance on gun rights to be any part of the "change" he promises.

But the nagging problem for so many gun owners is that the party leadership, and those in power positions within the party, have not simply dismissed gun owners, but instead declared a personal war against them.

In short, there is no evidence to suggest that Barack Obama or any other high-profile Democrat, would counsel fellow Democrats to change course in their relentless pursuit of increasingly restrictive gun control. If there were such people, there is no indication their party would listen. There is ample reason to believe that the "party of gun control" would need to shed a lot of political weight, in state legislatures and in governors' offices.

Let's take a brief look at some of the party's hardcore anti-gunners whose personal opinions currently, and most assuredly in the future, will dictate Democrat party policy and philosophy toward private gun ownership and firearm civil rights.

Sen. Joseph Biden of Delaware has twice run for president but never made it through the primaries. Rated "F" by the NRA for his consistent anti-gun stances, Biden voted against legislation to protect gun makers from harassment lawsuits, he would reinstate a ban on semiautomatic firearms that look like military rifles, and he supports legislation that would attack gun shows by closing a so-called "gun show loophole" that, according to a study done for the Department of Justice, essentially does not exist.

Wisconsin Gov. James Edward "Jim" Doyle perhaps exemplifies what may be wrong at the gubernatorial level. While biographical information from his 2002 campaign website insists that he "was an early public supporter of the proposed constitutional amendment to hunt, fish and trap," the actual right to keep and bear arms amendment now part of the Wisconsin constitution reads, "The people have the right to keep and bear arms for security, defense, hunting, recreation or any other lawful purpose."

Doyle's read of that language seems a bit selective, leaving out that bit about security and defense. He twice vetoed legislation that would have set up a concealed carry system in Wisconsin. Anything he says now about supporting the state and U.S. Constitutional right to keep and bear is empty rhetoric.

A close Doyle ally is Milwaukee Mayor Tom Barrett, a staunch supporter of tougher gun laws. He was an early backer of Barack Obama, and he lobbied Doyle hard to veto concealed carry legislation. He was also one of the first mayors to join the anti-gun "Mayors Against Illegal Guns" group.

New Jersey Gov. Jon Corzine is an extremist anti-gunner who left the U.S. Senate to run for the Garden State governorship. He has infuriated gun owners and hunters in New Jersey for ordering that state's wildlife managers to scrap a black bear hunt in an effort to reduce a growing bear population.

On measures strictly dealing with gun rights, Corzine favors licensing and registration of privately-owned firearms, he would ban so-called "Saturday Night Specials" (while nobody has ever really defined what kind of gun that is), and he would ban full-capacity ammunition magazines, and add restrictive regulations on handgun sales.

Another Democrat governor, Pennsylvania's Ed Rendell, is a veteran anti-gun rights zealot. His sentiments run toward limiting handgun sales to one per month (he lobbied the Pennsylvania legislature to pass such a law in 2007, but the idea was rejected), and he is an opponent of state preemption laws that prohibit cities and towns from enacting their own local gun ordinances, creating a nightmare patchwork of laws designed to ensnare gun owners and convict them of gun crimes, which would disqualify them from owning firearms.

He also wanted a law that would require gun owners to report lost or stolen guns immediately, or face criminal penalties, again disqualifying those citizens from ever again owning a firearm.

Rendell's anti-gun posturing dates back to his days as Philadelphia mayor, and the current mayor of that city, Michael Nutter, is a chip off that old anti-gun block. Reluctant, to take on violent gang crime, he deliberately signed ordinances that challenged Pennsylvania's preemption statute.

Among the laws he signed were a prohibition on so-called "assault weapons" in the city. He also signed an ordinance requiring people to report lost or stolen guns within 24 hours, and a one-gun-a-month law. Less than two months later, a Pennsylvania court issued a permanent restraining order against enforcement of two of those measures, the "assault weapon" ban and the once-per-month limit on handgun purchases.

But Nutter has promised to keep trying, and despite his promises to "talk to anyone" in an effort to fight out-of-control violent crime, he apparently forgot to include anyone from the gun rights community, such as representatives from the National Rifle Association (NRA), Citizens Committee for the Right to Keep and Bear Arms (CCRKBA), or Pennsylvania gun groups in those discussions. An NRA attorney went so far as to label Nutter a "tyrant" when the battle over gun laws erupted, while Nutter accused the NRA of being "virtually criminal" in its opposition to his anti-gun legislation.

Nutter is cut from the same cloth as Washington, D.C. Mayor Adrian Fenty, who aggressively defended that city's ban on handguns, all the way to the U.S. Supreme Court. His argument was that the Second Amendment did not apply to citizens, and even if it did, it did not apply to residents of the District of Columbia, because the District is not a state with a militia.

Then there is New Orleans Mayor Ray Nagin, who will forever be remembered as the man who presided over, and then defended, the unconstitutional confiscation of private firearms in the wake of Hurricane Katrina in 2005. Nagin's administration stonewalled against a federal lawsuit filed by the NRA and Second Amendment Foundation (SAF) to stop the gun seizures, initially denying they ever happened. Nagin has never apologized for the gun seizures, many of them accomplished at gunpoint against unsuspecting citizens.

Far-Left San Francisco Mayor Gavin Newsom and members of the San Francisco Board of Supervisors also fail to offer gun owners any semblance of rationality on the gun rights issue. Newsom became the second San Francisco mayor to lose a court case challenging a gun ban in that city; Dianne Feinstein was first, in 1982, when she pushed a ban that was quickly struck down in a case filed by the Second Amendment Foundation.

Incredibly, the more recent San Francisco debacle never had to happen, if only Newsom and the Board had heeded the vows of the NRA, SAF and CCRKBA to file a lawsuit if the city put an anti-gun initiative on its November 2005 ballot and it passed.

Within 48 hours of the election, NRA and SAF were joined by the Law Enforcement Alliance of America, the Association of California Firearms Retailers and private citizens in a lawsuit that followed the same path as the 1982 legal battle that SAF had waged on its own. The result was identical.

Illinois Gov. Rod Blagojevich is a former member of Congress who never met a gun control measure he did not immediately love. He has had to temper his anti-gun zeal a bit in the interest of down-state Democrats who could face stiff Republican opposition in conservative districts, but he is an ally of vehemently anti-gun Chicago Mayor Richard Daley.

The distance in miles between Blagojevich's native Chicago and Seattle, where Chicago-born liberal Democrat Greg Nickels now reigns as mayor, belies the close philosophical ties that Nickels has with the anti-gun Chicago political machine.

Another participant in Bloomberg's "Mayors Against Illegal Guns" (he was one of the charter members), it appears from his actions that Nickels believes all guns should be illegal. In June 2008, using a bizarre incident that occurred at Seattle's annual Folklife Festival as a launch pad, Nickels announced that he was going to ban all firearms, even those legally carried by licensed gun owners, from all city property by "executive order." That means his ban was not subject to city council review.

Nickels represents the worst of the Liberal mindset that is continually pulling the Democrat Party ever farther to the left. He is a fanatic. In the gun control arena, he has asked the Legislature to crack down on gun shows and enact bans on semiautomatic firearms. He has wanted to devastate Washington's long-standing preemption law since becoming mayor, and he is closely allied with Washington CeaseFire, the small but vocal extremist anti-gun organization.

Ohio's junior United States Senator, Sherrod Brown, is yet another Democrat whose left-leaning philosophy puts him in a position to influence the party's direction. An "F"-rated politician by the NRA, Brown twice voted against legislation that outlawed junk lawsuits against gun makers, in 2003 and 2005, while he was serving in the U.S. House of Representatives for Ohio's 13th District. He was elected to the Senate in 2006.

For many gun owners who have battled "the party of gun control" for years, it will require a public repudiation of gun control as a cornerstone Democrat issue. As a party, Democrats have their own generation of political dinosaurs who cling to the notion that gun ownership should be a regulated privilege rather than a fundamental individual civil right.

However, as demonstrated above, the eventual departures of people like Dianne Feinstein, Edward M. Kennedy, Charles Schumer, Bill and Hillary Clinton, Barbara Boxer, Patty Murray and John Kerry may leave voids, but there are many other Democrats with equal disdain for the rights of firearms owners jut waiting in the wings to fill their shoes.

And those dogs don't hunt, either.